READING AND WRITING Sourcebook

Authors

Robert Pavlik

Richard G. Ramsey

Great Source Education Group

a Houghton Mifflin Company

Wilmington, Massachusetts

Authors

Richard G. Ramsey is currently a national educational consultant for many schools throughout the country and serves as President of Ramsey's Communications. For more than twenty-three years he has served as a teacher and a principal for grades 1–12. Dr. Ramsey has also served on the Curriculum Frameworks Committee for the State of Florida. A lifelong teacher and educator and former principal, he is now a nationally known speaker on improving student achievement and motivating students.

Robert Pavlik taught high school English and reading for seven years. His university assignments in Colorado and Wisconsin have included teaching secondary/content area reading, chairing a Reading/Language Arts Department, and directing a Reading/Learning Center. He is an author of several books and articles and serves as the Director of the School of Design Center at Marquette University.

Printed in the United States of America.

International Standard Book Number: 0-669-47133-X

1 2 3 4 5 6 7 8 9 10 — BA — 05 04 03 02 01 00 99

Table of Contents

Table of Contents

Introduction

Responding to Literature   PAGES **8-10**

"Ain't I a Woman?" SPEECH   **Sojourner Truth**   8

"Letter to Samuel Mather" LETTER   **Benjamin Franklin**   10

Contemporary Issues

Identity   PAGES **11-32**

writing a paragraph   1. "The Good Daughter" ESSAY   **Caroline Hwang**   12

writing a narrative paragraph   2. "Bridges" AUTOBIOGRAPHY   **Walter Dean Myers**   21

Subjects: World History

World War I   PAGES **33-48**

writing a letter   3. "Pilots' Reflections" NONFICTION   **Robert Hull**   34

writing a summary   4. "Adventures of the U-202" NONFICTION   **Baron Spiegel**   42

Literature

Gwendolyn Brooks   PAGES **49-64**

writing a descriptive paragraph   5. "you're being so good, so kind," from *Maud Martha* FICTION   **Gwendolyn Brooks**   50

writing a descriptive paragraph   6. "Maud Martha and New York," from *Maud Martha* FICTION   **Gwendolyn Brooks**   57

環球
大酒樓

Contemporary Issues

New Lands   PAGES **65–84**

writing a poem   7. "Legal Alien" and "Immigrants" POEMS   **Pat Mora**   66

writing a review   8. "A Simple Proposition,"   **Lensey Namioka**   73
                         from *Who's Hu* FICTION

Subjects: Mythology

Myths and Monsters   PAGES **85–110**

writing a story   9. "The Cyclops' Cave" MYTH   **Bernard Evslin**   86

writing a descriptive 10. "Hercules" MYTH   **Edith Hamilton**   99
paragraph

Literature

Dorothy West   PAGES **111–124**

writing a compare   11. "The Richer, the Poorer" STORY   **Dorothy West**   112
and contrast paragraph

writing a paragraph   12. "The Richer, the Poorer" CONTINUED   **Dorothy West**   119

Contemporary Issues

▪ Protest and Revolt

PAGES **125-144**

writing a character description 13. "Animals Unite!" **George Orwell** 126
from *Animal Farm* FICTION

writing a journal entry 14. "The Fast," from **Mohandas K. Gandhi** 136
An Autobiography AUTOBIOGRAPHY

Subjects: Geography

▪ Africa

PAGES **145-160**

writing a summary 15. "A Sea of Dunes" NONFICTION **Jim Brandenburg** 146
writing an article 16. "The Widows of the Reserves" NONFICTION **Phyllis Ntantala** 153

Literature

▪ Luis Rodriguez

PAGES **161-176**

writing an autobiographical paragraph 17. "Ramiro," from **Luis Rodriguez** 161
Always Running AUTOBIOGRAPHY

writing a character description 18. "Ramiro," from **Luis Rodriguez** 171
Always Running CONTINUED

Contemporary Issues

■ **Conflict**   PAGES **177–196**

writing a paragraph 19. "Refusing Service," from   **Zora Neale Hurston**   178
of opinion   *Dust Tracks on a Road* AUTOBIOGRAPHY

writing an article   20. "Time to Look and Listen" ESSAY   **Magdoline Asfahani**   187

Subjects: World History

■ **World War II—The Holocaust**   PAGES **197–218**

writing a letter   21. "A Soldier's Letter Home" LETTER   **Delbert Cooper**   198

writing a journal entry 22. "Good-bye," from   **Gerta Weismann Klein**   206
                          All But My Life AUTOBIOGRAPHY

Literature

■ **Kurt Vonnegut**   PAGES **219–238**

writing a 3-paragraph essay 23. "Harrison Bergeron" STORY   **Kurt Vonnegut**   220

writing an episode   24. "The Kid Nobody Could Handle" STORY   **Kurt Vonnegut**   228

■ **Acknowledgments**   **239**

■ **Index**   **240**

READING AND WRITING Sourcebook

Do you talk to the text as you read? How do you respond to it? Watch what good readers do. Often they read with a pen in hand, marking lines of text, circling words, underlining phrases, and asking questions in the margins. You can read this way, too. It's easy to do, and it will help you understand more of what you read.

   Here's an example. Read the brief speech. Then look at the way the passage has been marked up.

RESPONSE NOTES

1. MARK ?? ─ "Ain't I a Woman?" by Sojourner Truth

2. QUESTION
   When did she write this?

3. CLARIFY
   She's saying she's equal to a man.

4. VISUALIZE
   woman
   man
   really?

5. PREDICT
   I bet people were surprised by what she said.

6. REACT
   I agree 100%!

May I say a few words? I want to say a few words about this matter. I am a woman's rights. I have as much muscle as any man, and can do as much work as any man. I have plowed and reaped and husked and chopped and mowed, and can any man do more than that? I have heard much about the sexes being equal. I can carry as much as any man, and can eat as much too, if I can get it. I am as strong as any man that is now. As for intellect, all I can say is, if woman have a pint, and man a quart—why can't she have her little pint full? You need not be afraid to give us our rights for fear we will take too much,—for we can't take more than our pint'll hold. The poor men seem to be all in confusion, and don't know what to do. Why children, if you have woman's rights, give it to her and you will feel better. You will have your own rights, and they won't be so much trouble. I can't read, but I can hear. I have heard the bible and have learned that Eve caused man to sin. Well, if woman upset the world, do give her a chance to set it right side up again. . . .

VOCABULARY
husked—took the outer covering, or husks, off corn.
Eve—referring to Adam and Eve of the Garden of Eden.

You can respond to a text in many ways. In fact, there is no one right way. Here are six general ways readers respond.

1. Mark or Highlight
With a pen, underline or circle words that are important or seem confusing. With a colorful marker, go over parts of a reading. By marking part of a text, you set off important parts of the text and make these parts easier to find.

2. Question
Form questions as you read. Ask questions such as, "Do I do this?" and ask questions of the author, such as, "Is this true?" This is a way of talking with the author. It triggers thoughts in your mind and makes the reading more meaningful.

3. Clarify
"What does this mean?" You probably ask that question as you read. We try to make clear to ourselves what we have read. Often we will put a thought in our own words—for example, "This means surrender." Other times we might number or label parts of a text to keep track of events in the plot, arguments an author is making, or connections from one page to another.

4. Visualize
When you read, you see mental pictures of what the writer is describing. To help remember these mental pictures, you can also draw what you see. You may make a chart or organizer or draw a picture or sketch. Any of these ways of visualizing are useful.

5. Predict
Another common way of responding to literature is to guess what will happen next. "How will this story come out in the end?" Readers make predictions as they read. It is a way of keeping interest in a selection and giving a reason to read and finish a story or article.

6. React and Connect
Readers often sound off, jotting notes and comments in the margins of books. This, too, is a way of getting more from your reading. It helps you state your own views by noting them as you read.

Use these strategies in the Response Notes space beside each selection in this *Sourcebook*. Look back at these examples if you need to. Try some of them yourself on the selection below.

Mark it up any way you want, but try to use at least 2 or 3 response strategies.

RESPONSE NOTES

"Letter to Samuel Mather" by Benjamin Franklin

May 12, 1784

Rev. Sir,

I received your kind letter with your excellent advice to the people of the United States, which I read with great pleasure, and hope it will be duly regarded. Such writings, though they may be lightly passed over by many readers, yet, if they make a deep impression on one active mind in a hundred, the effects may be considerable. Permit me to mention one little instance, which, though it relates to myself, will not be quite uninteresting to you. When I was a boy, I met with a book, entitled "Essays to do Good," which I think was written by your father. It had been so little regarded by a former possessor, that several leaves of it were torn out; but the remainder gave me such a turn of thinking, as to have an influence on my conduct throughout life; for I have always set a greater value on the character of a doer of good, than on any other kind of reputation; and if I have been, as you seem to think, a useful citizen, the public owes the advantage of it to that book.

B. Franklin

Identity

What kind of person are you? How do you define who you are? Is your identity based on . . .

beliefs?

friends?

accomplishments?

family?

appearances?

1: The Good Daughter

Ever feel torn about which way to go or who your true self is? Look for a connection between yourself and what you read. One way to connect is to do a quickwrite.

BEFORE YOU READ

Read the title of the essay and the opening paragraphs on the next page.

1. Decide, "What is this about?"

2. Ask yourself, "What experience in my life does it remind me of?"

3. Quickwrite about your experience for 1 minute.

1-MINUTE QUICKWRITE

(topic) I think "The Good Daughter" is about . . .

(your memories) I remember a time . . .

II. READ

Read "The Good Daughter."

1. As you read, underline information about Caroline.

2. Circle information about her parents and write any **questions** you have in the Response Notes.

"The Good Daughter" by Caroline Hwang

The moment I walked into the dry-cleaning store, I knew the woman behind the counter was from Korea, like my parents. To show her that we shared a heritage, and possibly get a fellow countryman's discount, I tilted my head forward, in shy imitation of a traditional bow.

"Name?" she asked, not noticing my attempted obeisance.

"Hwang," I answered.

"Hwang? Are you Chinese?"

Her question caught me off-guard. I was used to hearing such queries from non-Asians who think Asians all look alike, but never from one of my own people. Of course, the only Koreans I knew were my parents and their friends, people who've never asked me where I came from, since they knew better than I.

I ransacked my mind for the Korean words that would tell her who I was. It's always struck me as funny (in a mirthless sort of way) that I can more readily say "I am Korean" in Spanish, German and even Latin than I can in the language of my ancestry. In the end, I told her in English.

VOCABULARY
Korea—country in East Asia.
discount—lesser amount than the usual or full price.
traditional—passed down from one generation to another.
obeisance—act of honoring.
queries—questions.
ransacked—searched thoroughly.
mirthless—humorless, serious.
ancestry—of one's ancestors, or grandparents and great-grandparents.

RESPONSE NOTES

EXAMPLE:
Korean parents

13

The dry-cleaning woman squinted as though trying to see past the glare of my strangeness, repeating my surname under her breath. "Oh, *Fxuang*," she said, doubling over with laughter. "You don't know how to speak your name."

I flinched. Perhaps I was particularly sensitive at the time, having just dropped out of graduate school. I had torn up my map for the future, the one that said not only where I was going but who I was. My sense of identity was already disintegrating.

How did the dry cleaner's words affect Caroline?

_____

_____

_____

When I got home, I called my parents to ask why they had never bothered to correct me. "Big deal," my mother said, sounding more flippant than I knew she intended. (Like many people who learn English in a classroom, she uses idioms that don't always fit the occasion.) "So what if you can't pronounce your name? You are American," she said.

Though I didn't challenge her explanation, it left me unsatisfied. The fact is, my cultural identity is hardly that clear-cut.

My parents immigrated to this country 30 years ago, two years before I was born. They told me often, while I was growing up, that, if I wanted to, I could be president someday, that here my grasp would be as long as my reach.

VOCABULARY

squinted—looked with eyes partly closed.
flinched—started or winced suddenly, as if out of surprise or pain.
disintegrating—falling apart.
flippant—casual; lighthearted.
idioms—figures of speech or expressions with a special meaning, such as "It's raining cats and dogs."

To ensure that I reaped all the advantages of this country, my parents saw to it that I became fully <u>assimilated</u>. So, like any American of my generation, I whiled away my youth strolling malls and talking on the phone, <u>rhapsodizing</u> over Andrew McCarthy's blue eyes or analyzing the meaning of a certain upperclassman's offer of a ride to the Homecoming football game.

STOP AND THINK

What 2–3 things have you learned so far about Caroline?

_____

_____

_____

To my parents, I am all American, and the sacrifices they made in leaving Korea—including my mispronounced name—pale in comparison to the opportunities those sacrifices gave me. They do not see that I <u>straddle</u> two cultures, nor that I feel displaced in the only country I know. I identify with Americans, but Americans do not identify with me. I've never known what it's like to belong to a community—neither one at large, nor of an extended family. I know more about Europe than the continent my ancestors unmistakably come from. I sometimes wonder, as I did that day in the dry cleaner's, if I would be a happier person had my parents stayed in Korea.

I first began to consider this thought around the time I decided to go to graduate school. It had been a compromise: my parents wanted me to go to law school; I wanted to skip the <u>starched-collar track</u> and be a writer—the hungrier the better. But after 20-some

VOCABULARY
assimilated—became like members of a larger group (like Americans).
rhapsodizing—speaking or writing emotionally.
straddle—stand or sit with a leg on each side of.
starched-collar track—life of middle-class business people who work in offices.

15

years of following their wishes and meeting all of their expectations, I couldn't bring myself to disobey or disappoint. A writing career is riskier than law, I remember thinking. If I'm a failure and my life is a washout, then what does that make my parents' lives?

I know that many of my friends had to choose between pleasing their parents and being true to themselves. But for the children of immigrants, the choice seems more complicated, a happy outcome impossible. By making the biggest move of their lives for me, my parents indentured me to the largest debt imaginable—I owe them the fulfillment of their hopes for me.

It tore me up inside to suppress my dream, but I went to school for a Ph.D. in English literature, thinking I had found the perfect compromise. I would be able to write at least about books while pursuing a graduate degree. Predictably, it didn't work out. How could I labor for five years in a program I had no passion for? When I finally left school, my parents were disappointed, but since it wasn't what they wanted me to do, they weren't devastated. I, on the other hand, felt I was staring at the bottom of the abyss. I had seen the flaw in my life of halfwayness, in my planned life of compromises.

STOP AND THINK

Why did Caroline feel like she let down her parents?

_____

_____

_____

VOCABULARY
indentured—bound into service, enslaved.
compromise—settlement of differences in which each side gives up something.
abyss—immeasurable or profound depth.

I hadn't thought about my love life, but I had a vague plan to make concessions there, too. Though they raised me as an American, my parents expect me to marry someone Korean and give them grandchildren who look like them. This didn't seem like such a huge request when I was 14, but now I don't know what I'm going to do. I've never been in love with someone I dated, or dated someone I loved. (Since I can't bring myself even to entertain the thought of marrying the non-Korean men I'm attracted to, I've been dating only those I know I can stay clearheaded about.) And as I near that age when the question of marriage stalks every relationship, I can't help but wonder if my parents' expectations are responsible for the lack of passion in my life.

My parents didn't want their daughter to be Korean, but they don't want her fully American, either. Children of immigrants are living paradoxes. We are the first generation and the last. We are in this country for its opportunities, yet filial duty binds us. When my parents boarded the plane, they knew they were embarking on a rough trip. I don't think they imagined the rocks in the path of their daughter who can't even pronounce her own name.

STOP AND THINK

What does Caroline consider "the rocks in the path" of her life?

_____

_____

_____

VOCABULARY
concessions—points or things given up reluctantly, as part of a negotiation.
stalks—haunts or pursues.
paradoxes—statements that seem to not make sense but are in fact true.
filial—of or relating to a son or daughter.

A. COMPARE Look again at the way you marked up the essay. What have you learned about Caroline? What have you learned about her parents?

CAROLINE WANTS TO BE...	THE HWANGS WANT CAROLINE TO BE...
1.	
2.	
3.	

B. LIMIT THE TOPIC Next, think about a topic to write about. Make the topic something about finding an identity. Then make it smaller so it will be easier to write about.

Topic

C. SUPPORT THE TOPIC Choose one of the narrowed topics and write 3 details about it.

Topic:

1.

2.

3.

IV. WRITE

Now write a **paragraph** about finding an identity.

1. Begin with a sentence that describes your topic. This will be your topic sentence.
2. Then add a sentence for each of the details you listed on the previous page. These sentences will support the topic sentence and provide the kinds of support that make your writing believable and interesting.
3. Use the Writers' Checklist below to help you revise.

WRITERS' CHECKLIST

SENTENCES

☐ Did your sentences always begin with a capital letter?
☐ Did your sentences always end with a punctuation mark?
☐ Did your sentences always express a complete thought?
Example: *Caroline struggled to find her identity.*

日用百貨
兒童玩具
各種吊食
精工藝品

Successful readers visualize what they read. This means that they make mental pictures of the characters, setting, and action. Sometimes reading aloud can help you "see" a story more clearly.

BEFORE YOU READ

Divide into small groups of 3 or 4.

1. Take turns reading each sentence below. Then decide what order you think the sentences appear in Walter Dean Myers's memoir, "Bridges."

2. Then discuss, after reading the sentences, what you think it will be about.

"'I think you're getting old,' he said smiling. 'You're sounding a lot like Grandpa.'"

"Then he was ill. Then he was dying."

"My wife had grown to care for my father, accepting his irascible ways . . ."

"I needed his final approval, his blessing if you will, of the man I had become."

THINK–PAIR–AND–SHARE

II. READ

Stay in your group and take turns reading aloud. When you come to a "Stop and Think" box, it's time to switch readers.

1. At that point, take a moment to sketch the people and places you've been reading about.

2. As you read, **highlight** passages that surprise or interest you.

RESPONSE NOTES

"Bridges" by Walter Dean Myers

I was two and a half when the young woman who gave birth to me died, and not much older than that when I was sent to another family to be raised. I have no memory of the bus trip from West Virginia to Harlem, or of my first meeting with Herbert and Florence Dean, the only parents I have ever known. What I have known of these people, who I remember them to be, has changed over the years, coming most sharply into focus upon my father's death in 1986.

The last winter snow had finally melted and the tops of the trees were showing the first signs of new life when it became clear that he was failing. Each day my wife and I coaxed our old Maverick out to the East Orange Veteran's Hospital, the silence in the car was heavy with grief, for we knew that any visit might be the last. My wife had grown to care for my father, accepting his irascible ways and worrying about his diet much more than I ever did. Her visits to the hospital were selfless, filled with sympathy for both me and my father. My own concerns, viewed through the prism of distance, were not as pure. I, too, cursed the disease which had consumed his strength, which had destroyed this Black man from within as nothing had been able to do from without, but there was also something that I needed from him, one last gift before

EXAMPLE:
a great image!

VOCABULARY
coaxed—obtained by persuasion or pleading.
irascible—easily angered.
prism—lens or medium that distorts slightly.

he went on his way. I needed his final approval, his blessing if you will, of the man I had become.

From my own <u>maturity</u> my father was an easy man to understand. Hard times were normal for Blacks in Baltimore, where he was born in 1907. By the age of 10 he was working full-time. His father was a tall, Bible-willed man who ran a horse and wagon hauling business, and when my father was a child his grandfather, in Virginia, still worked the land on which he had once been enslaved.

Like other poor children his age in those pre-World War I days, he found that good times and full bellies were few and far between. He developed a clear, useful wisdom. If you weren't willing to work for something, you really didn't want it. It was a philosophy, imprinted on him as he hauled wood through the streets of Baltimore, that both colored and shaped his life.

My Dad wasn't a man to take a lot of nonsense. He found himself in court as a teenager for knocking down a White southerner who ordered him off the sidewalk as the man's wife passed. He found himself in jail for shooting at a man who tried to cheat him out of a day's wages.

STOP AND THINK

What I've learned about Mr. Dean:

Sketch

VOCABULARY
maturity—time of being fully developed physically.

My <u>adoptive</u> mother had to be the best looking woman he ever met. Or is that my memory? Half Indian, half German, from a little community near Lancaster, Pennsylvania, Florence Gearhart had worked as a cook's helper from the time she was 13. What they had in common, I think, was the understanding of what it was to be poor in America, and the <u>ambition</u> to do better.

The decision to move to New York must have been an exciting one for them. My mother talked of her early days in Harlem as overwhelming. My father had done some work on the docks in Baltimore and quickly found the New York waterfront. It was easier for Blacks to get night work and he worked the docks when he could in the evenings and worked on one of the <u>mobster</u> Dutch Schultz's moving vans during the day. Mama did days work, cleaning homes. She used to tell me about the first years of their marriage with an excitement that escaped me. I didn't understand why my father would get mad because some piano player named Fats Waller paid Mama too much attention, or why she would get mad if he lost money gambling with a tap dancer by the name of Bojangles.

In my family there were no psychological <u>inducements</u> to behave properly. There were simply standards one learned by a tone of voice, a raised eyebrow, a significant pause. You respected all adults you met. You did not associate with anyone unworthy of respect. In the home you <u>refrained</u> from backtalk—and backtalk included sucking one's teeth, rolling one's eyes, and fixing one's mouth as if one wanted to say something fresh.

VOCABULARY

adoptive—related by adoption, as opposed to by birth.
ambition—desire to achieve fame or fortune.
mobster—member of a criminal gang.
inducements—influences or incentives.
refrained—held back.

When my mother wasn't out working she was working around the house. She seemed to be always washing, dusting, or <u>ironing</u> something. I would follow her from room to room, as she never seemed to tire of talking to me. In the afternoon, the work done and the dinner started, she would read to me from *True Romances*. The heavy bosoms didn't mean much to me, but the sound of her voice in that spotless, sun-drenched Harlem kitchen did.

STOP AND THINK

What I know about Mrs. Dean:	Sketch

There was never a moment when a light bulb went off and I announced to the world that I could read. But somehow, by the time I was five, I was reading. I could handle *True Romances* all by myself.

By the time I reached Junior High School 43, I was officially listed as "bright." The reading that had begun with *True Romances* and comic books expanded. I read <u>voraciously</u>. I had begun to write. I had also begun to grow farther and farther away from my parents.

Why? What happened between us? I had changed, had grown through books and reading in ways unfamiliar to my parents.

VOCABULARY

ironing—pressing and smoothing clothes with a heated iron.
voraciously—greedily, with an appetite that seemingly cannot be satisfied.

High school brought new opportunities, and new problems. My tenth-grade reading included Thomas Mann, Honoré de Balzac, Eugene O'Neill, and Dylan Thomas. Reading was excellent to me, and so, increasingly, was writing. Dealing with ideas became an overt part of my consciousness. But there were other influences, viewed now from adult understanding, which affected me greatly. My father was working as a janitor/handyman. Everyone in the tenement in which I lived worked with their hands at menial jobs.

My parents began to represent to me what I did not want to be. I began to find my identity in the books and in the concept of myself as an "intellectual." Being "smart" became the refuge from the notion of the Black inferiority that was being offered to me in school and in the general society and which I had, unconsciously, accepted. I was crushed when I discovered that I would not be able to go to college.

It had been a sacrifice for my parents to maintain me in high school, and they simply could not afford to keep a growing young man in school, without help. In a fit of teenaged angst, I dropped out of school. I welcomed the trouble to be found in the streets of Harlem, deliberately defying the family tenets, rejecting the values I felt had rejected me. In effect, I dropped out of my father's world.

My father and I became cautious friends when I reached my mid-20s, and closer friends after my mother died. But still there was a gap between us, a distance between us that I couldn't understand. I had overcome

VOCABULARY
Thomas Mann—German novelist who lived from 1875–1955.
Honoré de Balzac—French novelist who lived from 1788–1868.
Eugene O'Neill—American playwright who lived from 1888–1953.
Dylan Thomas—Welsh poet who lived from 1914–53.
tenement—run-down, low-rental apartment building.
menial—appropriate for a servant.
inferiority—sense of feeling undervalued or being lesser or lower valued.
angst—feeling of anxiety or depression.
tenets—beliefs or principles.

"Bridges" continued

my juvenile hostility/rebellion, and it was my father who now seemed distant. In particular I felt that he wasn't pleased with my writing. Yet, as I began to be published, that's who I was, and how I identified myself.

Still, we got on. He seemed to enjoy my company. We spent holidays together, and he helped me with a hundred house repairs. But he never mentioned the books I wrote.

Then he was ill. Then he was dying. Then I was sitting by his hospital bed, seeking the last approval, seeking the last blessing.

I brought my new books to the hospital room. I brought him stories of what I was doing. I said the words "I love you," and punctuated them with my tears. When he returned my declaration of love, I wanted to ask him if he also loved my books, if he also loved the writer I had become. I never did. Words seemed inadequate. What did "I love you" mean when the words were so expected? What did they mean when they echoed from antiseptic hospital walls but missed the uneasy contours of our relationship?

STOP AND THINK

What I know about the narrator: | Sketch

VOCABULARY
juvenile—not fully grown or developed; young.
contours—outlines or shapes.

Sitting in my father's empty house after his death was hard. There were a thousand reminders of special moments gone by. The old cowboy belt he let me play with as a child but would never give me. The New Testament he had given me when, on my 17th birthday, I had joined the army. But it was his papers that fascinated me most. As I went through them I was shocked. I looked at them over and over, turning them in my hands, wondering why I had never guessed his secret before.

I remembered him coming to my house, asking me to read some document to him, saying that he had misplaced his glasses. I recalled him sitting at a table asking me to check if an insurance form was "filled out right" or if he had "signed in all the right places." My father couldn't read well enough to handle my books.

When I was a child my father talked to me, told me absurdly wonderful stories. It was these stories that allowed me to release the balloon of my imagination, and to let it soar. It was his stories, and those of my grandfather, that gave me permission to tell stories myself, to think it was the thing I wanted to do. I was allowed to take the  world of the imagination and make it my own. It was my mother, reading her magazines, that furthered that imagination, gave it order, defined it more in words than pictures.

VOCABULARY

insurance—coverage by a contract that agrees to pay money in the event of an injury, illness, or death.
permission—consent or agreement for doing something.

"Bridges" continued

Herbert and Florence Dean were bridges I have crossed over. Bridges from the harder time they knew to the better time they did not know. They were willing to take me to the shores they weren't able to manage themselves, and bid me Godspeed.

I wish I had known my father couldn't read while he was alive. I would have told him my stories. I would have *read* to him the stories I had written, the same stories that he had once told me. But those times have passed and I'll take from them, and from what I have learned from them. That I, too, have stories to pass on and advice to give and a critical eye grounded in my own time and space.

My youngest boy was going for an interview recently. He's quite the young man now and fairly sure of himself. Despite my best intentions not to, I gave him all the advice I had promised myself I would withhold. "I think you're getting old," he said smiling. "You're sounding a lot like Grandpa."

It was one of the nicest things he's ever said to me.

STOP AND THINK

What I know about the Dean family:

Sketch

GATHER YOUR THOUGHTS

DISCUSS Stay in your reading group. Have a group discussion of the story.

1. A group leader should get the discussion started (and keep it moving).
2. Ask some open-ended questions, such as the ones below.
3. Write your ideas about each question.

DISCUSSION GUIDE

"BRIDGES"

Discussion Question #1

WHAT IS YOUR REACTION TO WALTER DEAN MYERS'S STORY?

My notes:

Discussion Question #2

IN WHAT WAYS DOES THE DEAN FAMILY REMIND YOU OF YOUR OWN?

My notes:

Discussion Question #3

WHAT EVENT OR EVENTS FROM YOUR OWN LIFE ARE SIMILAR TO THE EVENTS MYERS DESCRIBES?

My notes:

DISCUSSION HINTS

- Be prepared.
- Be willing to listen.
- Be willing to share.
- Build on one another's ideas.

©GREAT SOURCE. COPYING IS PROHIBITED.

WRITE

Use your discussion notes to help you write a **personal experience paragraph.** Tell about an important event for your family. You be the narrator of your story.

1. Put the name of the event in the title.
2. Begin your paragraph the same way that Myers begins "Bridges."
3. When you're done, use the Writers' Checklist to revise your paragraph.

Title: _____

I was _____ years old when _____ (name the event).

_____

_____

_____

_____

_____

_____

_____

_____

_____

_____

_____

_____

_____

_____

_____

_____

_____

WRITERS' CHECKLIST

SENTENCE FRAGMENTS

☐ **Did you avoid writing sentence fragments?**
A sentence fragment is a group of words that may start with a capital letter and finish with an end punctuation mark but is not a complete sentence.
To fix a fragment you may need to add a subject or a verb, eliminate or add words, or combine the fragment with another sentence.
EXAMPLES: When the man finished writing. (fragment)
When the man finished writing, he smiled. (sentence)
The man finished writing. (sentence)

Continue your writing on the next page.

Continue your writing from the previous page.

V. WRAP-UP

What did you learn from "Bridges"?

READERS' CHECKLIST

MEANING

- ❑ Did you learn something from the reading?
- ❑ Did it affect you or make an impression?

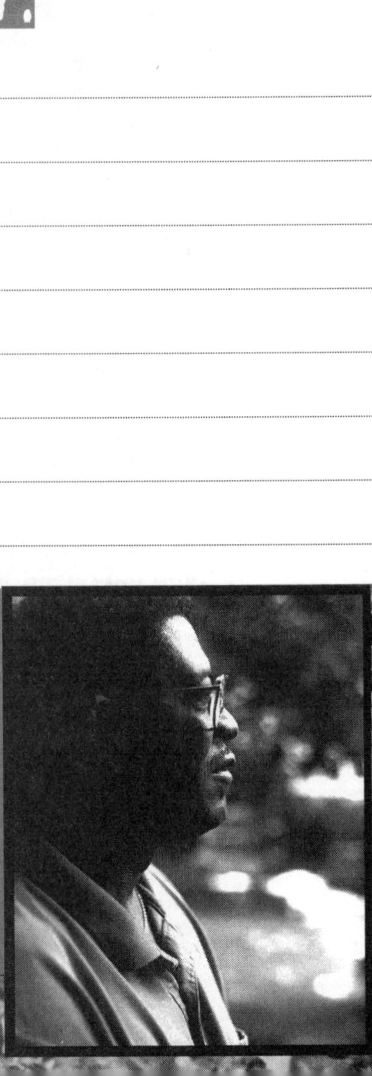

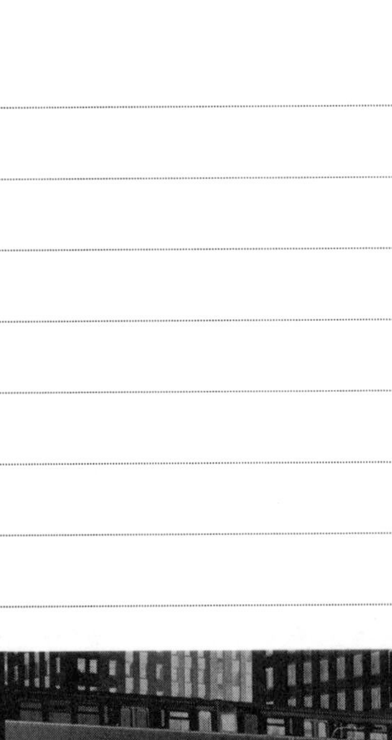

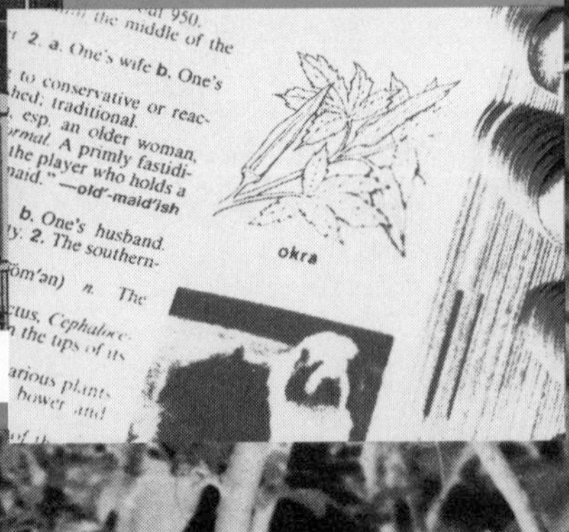

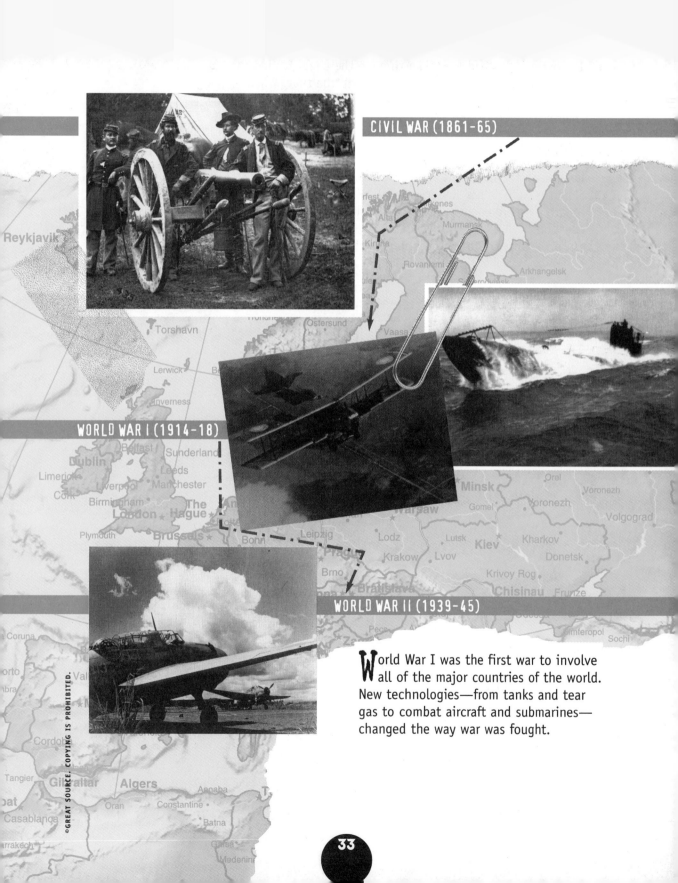

CIVIL WAR (1861–65)

WORLD WAR I (1914–18)

WORLD WAR II (1939–45)

Reykjavik

Torshavn

Lerwick

Inverness

Dublin
Belfast
Sunderland
Limerick
Leeds
Cork
Liverpool
Manchester
Birmingham
London
The Hague
Plymouth
Brussels
Bonn
Leipzig
Lodz
Lutsk
Kiev
Kharkov
Krakow
Lvov
Donetsk
Brno
Bratislava
Krivoy Rog
Chisinau
Frunze
Minsk
Voronezh
Gomel
Voronezh
Volgograd
Orel
Warsaw
Murmansk
Arkhangelsk
Kirkenes
Alta
Rovaniemi
Ostersund
Vaasa
Trondheim

Coruna
Porto
Val
Cordoba
Tangier
Gibraltar
Algers
Oran
Constantine
Casablanca
Batna
rrakech
Medenine
Sochi
Simferopol
Annaba

W orld War I was the first war to involve
all of the major countries of the world.
New technologies—from tanks and tear
gas to combat aircraft and submarines—
changed the way war was fought.

When you want to see a certain movie, you don't read all the listings. Instead, you skim through the paper to find the movie you want to see. Good readers skim all the time. When they read to answer questions, they don't read every word. Instead, they skim to find just the details that they need.

BEFORE YOU READ

Read through the questions about the selection below.

1. Skim through "Pilots' Reflections." Don't read every word. Look for key words and phrases that will help you answer the questions.

2. Write the answers to the questions in the space below.

SKIMMING

✔ How long ago was World War 1?

✔ How did countries use planes during the war?

✔ What did W. S. Douglas do when he saw an enemy plane?

II. READ

Now read the selection about two World War I pilots.
1. Circle at least 3 things about World War I.
2. Jot down any **questions** you have in the Response Notes.

"Pilots' Reflections" by Robert Hull (editor)

EDITOR'S NOTE: The 1914–1918 war was the first in which airplanes took part. They were very <u>fragile</u> things, made of wood and <u>canvas</u> and held together by wires. They flew only at about 50 miles (80 <u>kilometers</u>) per hour and couldn't go far. At the beginning of the war planes were used for <u>reconnaissance</u> and dropping bombs. It hardly occurred to fliers that they could use their planes to attack other planes. British wing-commander W. S. Douglas carried a rifle "for safety's sake."

The first time I ever encountered a German machine in the air, both the pilot (Harvey-Kelly) and myself were completely unarmed. Our machine had not been climbing well, and as I was considered somewhat heavy for an observer, Harvey-Kelly told me to leave behind all unnecessary gear. I therefore left behind my <u>carbine</u> and ammunition. We were taking photographs of the <u>trench</u> system to the north of Neuve Chapelle when I suddenly <u>espied</u> a German two-seater about 100 yards away and just below us. The German observer did not appear to be shooting at us. There was

VOCABULARY
fragile—easily broken.
canvas—heavy, coarse fabric or cloth used for tents and sails.
kilometers—unit of measurement equal to about two-thirds of a mile.
reconnaissance—exploration of an area to gather information.
carbine—lightweight rifle with a short barrel.
trench—long, narrow ditch.
espied—caught sight of.

RESPONSE NOTES

nothing to be done. We waved a hand to the enemy and proceeded with our task. The enemy did likewise. At the time this did not appear to me in any way ridiculous—there is a bond of sympathy between all who fly, even between enemies. But afterwards just for safety's sake I always carried a carbine with me in the air.

STOP AND THINK

Summarize what just happened.

Use your own words instead of the author's words.

Now read a diary entry that another pilot wrote during World War I.

When two pilots chased each other around the sky it seemed like an old-fashioned combat between two armed knights. Some fliers became famous, like the German Manfred von Richthofen. He described the end of a fight in the air in the diary he kept. He was shot down and died in 1918.

We were by now deep behind our lines at an altitude of about five hundred meters. I forced the Englishman to make more turns. While turning in an air fight one drops lower and lower until one must land, or attempt to fly straight home. My Englishman decided to do the latter. Lightning-quick the thought came to me: Now the hour for this poor fellow has come! I sat behind him. At the

VOCABULARY
Manfred von Richthofen—German pilot who gained fame during World War I.
altitude—height of a thing above sea level.

GREAT SOURCE. COPYING IS PROHIBITED.

"Pilots' Reflections" CONTINUED

necessary distance, about fifty meters away, I sighted him clearly and pressed my machine-gun buttons. What next! Not a shot came out. A jam in the guns. I cleared them and again pressed the machine-gun buttons: Not a shot! Curses! Success so near! I looked at my machine guns once more. Blast! I had already shot my last round. I have the empty ammunition belts in my hands. A thousand shots! I had used so many when I did not need them.

Under no <u>circumstances</u> could I allow him to get away, however.

To have fought with a red machine for almost a quarter of an hour and to have escaped—that would be a <u>triumph</u> for the English!

STOP aND THink

Summarize the problem von Richthofen faces.

_____

_____

_____

_____

I flew closer and closer to him, the distance from my propeller to his rudder constantly decreasing. I estimated: ten meters, five meters, three, now only two meters. Finally a <u>perplexing</u> thought came to me: Shall I strike his <u>rudder</u> with my <u>propeller</u>? Then he would fall,

RESPONSE NOTES

VOCABULARY
circumstances—conditions or facts about an event that have bearing on it.
triumph—victory or win.
perplexing—troubling or confusing.
rudder—tail of an aircraft used to change the direction of the plane.
propeller—blades that spin and are attached to the engine of an aircraft. They are used to push air and generate speed.

but I should probably go with him. Another thought: If I shut the engine off the minute I touch him, what would happen? Then my Englishman looked round at me, saw me directly behind him, cast a terrified glance at me, shut his engine off, and landed near our third position. Down on the ground he let his engine <u>idle</u>.

When a pilot lands near the enemy, he tries to set fire to his plane to destroy it. In order to prevent this, one shoots in the <u>vicinity</u> of the plane in such cases until the pilot runs away. So I flew over so close to his head that he noticed I was on the alert. The Englishman jumped out of his machine, waved to me and held his hands high, and let himself be taken by our infantry nearby.

VOCABULARY
idle—remain inactive.
vicinity—general area of or nearby.

stop and think

What did you learn about World War I?

_____

_____

_____

GATHER YOUR THOUGHTS

A. FIND THE MAIN IDEA The point the writer tries to make is the main idea.

1. Choose one of the two events to write about.

2. Write the main idea—the point the writer is trying to make—in the center circle. In the outer circles, write details from the selection. The details should "prove" the main idea.

detail

detail

The
writer wants to say

detail

detail

B. ORGANIZE DETAILS Now organize your thoughts before you begin writing a letter to a friend about the event the writer described. List at least 3 details in the order they occurred (#1 happened first, #2 happened next, and so on).

Main Idea

The event showed me . . .

Detail #1

Detail #2

Detail #3

IV. WRITE

Now put yourself back in the time during World War I. Imagine that you witnessed one of the events in this selection. Write a **letter** to a friend to tell about what you saw.

1. Begin with the main idea—the point that you want to make about the event.
2. Then include details to support your main idea.
3. Use the Writers' Checklist to help you revise.

Begin your letter with a greeting. Friendly letters usually begin with *Dear* followed by the name of the person to whom you are writing. Capitalize the name in the greeting and end with a comma.
EXAMPLES: *Dear Sarah,*
Dear Mrs. Gomez,

Dear _____

WRITERS' CHECKLIST

LETTERS

❑ Did your letter have an opening greeting and a closing?
❑ Did you use commas correctly in your greeting and closing?
❑ Did you begin the first word of the closing with a capital letter?
❑ Did you capitalize the name in the greeting?

End your letter with a closing. The first word of a closing begins with a capital letter. The closing ends with a comma.
EXAMPLES: *Yours truly,*
Sincerely, Best wishes,

V. WRAP-UP

Did you find the pilots' writings easy or hard to read? Why?

A good reader, instead of just starting right in, first prepares for reading. Look at the title and first part of the article or story. Think to yourself: What do I already know about this topic? What do I need to find out to understand it better? Some readers organize their thoughts in a K-W-L (What I **K**now – What I **W**ant to Know – What I **L**earned) chart.

 BEFORE YOU READ

Read the title and first paragraph of the article.

1. Think about what you already know about the topic and what you want to know.

2. Fill in the K and W sections in the chart below.

K-W-L CHART

K. Write what you already <u>know</u> about the topic.

– · – · – · – · – · – · – · – · – · – · – · –

W. Write what you <u>want</u> to know. Make a list of your questions.

– · – · – · – · – · – · – · – · – · – · – · –

L. Write what you <u>learned</u> after you read.

II. READ

Now read the rest of the article. As you read, keep the questions you wrote in the **W** space in the back of your mind.

1. Underline or circle parts that answer your questions.
2. When you read, you might think of new **questions**. Write them down in the Response Notes.

"Adventures of the U-202" by Baron Spiegel

Noiselessly we slipped closer and closer in our exciting chase. The main thing was that our periscope should not be observed, or the steamer might change her course at the last moment and escape us. Very cautiously, I stuck just the tip of the periscope above the surface at intervals of a few minutes, took the position of the steamer in a second and, like a flash, pulled it down again. That second was sufficient for me to see what I wanted to see. The steamer was to starboard and was heading at a good speed across our bows. To judge from the foaming waves which were cut off from the bow, I calculated that her speed must be about sixteen knots.

The hunter knows how important it is to have a knowledge of the speed at which his prey is moving. He can calculate the speed a little closer when it is a wounded hare than when it is one which in flight rushes past at high speed.

EXAMPLE:
How much of it was visible?

STOP AND PREDICT

What is going to happen?

VOCABULARY
periscope—device on a submarine used to see above water while the submarine is still below water.
steamer—large boat powered by steam, often used during the time of World War I to carry passengers across the ocean.
starboard—right-hand side of a ship as one faces forward.
bows—front parts of a ship or boat.
knots—units of speed equal to about 1.15 miles per hour.
prey—something hunted.
hare—animal similar to a rabbit.

It was only necessary for me, therefore, to calculate the speed of the ship for which a sailor has an experienced eye. I then plotted the exact angle we needed. I measured this by a scale which had been placed above the sights of the periscope. Now I only had to let the steamer come along until it had reached the zero point on the periscope and fire the torpedo, which then must strike its mark.

You see, it is very plain; I estimate the speed of the boat, aim with the periscope and fire at the right moment.

He who wishes to know about this or anything else in this connection should join the navy, or if he is not able to do so, send us his son or brother or nephew.

On the occasion in question everything went as calculated. The steamer could not see our cautious and hardly-shown periscope and continued unconcerned on its course. The diving rudder in the "Centrale" worked well and greatly facilitated my unobserved approach. I could clearly distinguish the various objects on board, and saw the giant steamer at a very short distance—how the captain was walking back and forth on the bridge with a short pipe in his mouth, how the crew was scrubbing the forward deck. I saw with amazement—a shiver went through me—a long line of compartments of wood spread over the entire deck, out of which were sticking black and brown horse heads and necks.

STOP AND PREDICT

Will the captain still torpedo the ship after seeing the horses? Why?

_____

_____

VOCABULARY

angle—figure formed by two lines that go from a single point.
torpedo—cigar-shaped underwater missile fired from a submarine.
nephew—son of one's brother or sister or of one's spouse's brother or sister.
rudder—plate mounted on the stern of a boat or ship and used for steering.
compartments—parts or spaces into which something is divided.

Oh, great Scott! Horses! What a pity! Splendid animals!

"What has that to do with it?" I continually thought. War is war. And every horse less on the western front is to lessen England's defense. I have to admit, however, that the thought which had to come was disgusting, and I wish to make the story about it short.

Only a few degrees were lacking for the desired angle, and soon the steamer would get into the correct focus. It was passing us at the right distance, a few hundred meters.

"Torpedo ready!" I called down into the "Centrale."

It was the longed-for command. Every one on board held his breath. Now the steamer's bow cut the line in the periscope—now the deck, the bridge, the <u>foremast</u>— the funnel.

"Let go!"

A light trembling shook the boat—the torpedo was on its way. Woe, when it was let loose!

There it was speeding, the murderous <u>projectile</u>, with an <u>insane</u> speed straight at its prey. I could accurately follow its path by the light wake it left in the water.

"Twenty seconds," counted the mate whose duty it was, with watch in hand, to calculate the exact time elapsed after the torpedo was fired until it exploded.

■ VOCABULARY ■
foremast—mast nearest the front of a sailing vessel.
projectile—object that is propelled, like a bullet or missile.
insane—crazy.

"Twenty-two seconds!"

Now it must happen—the terrible thing!

I saw the ship's people on the bridge had discovered the wake which the torpedo was leaving, a slender stripe. How they pointed with their fingers out across the sea in terror; how the captain, covering his face with his hands, resigned himself to what must come. And next there was a terrific shaking so that all aboard the steamer were tossed about and then, like a volcano, arose, majestic but fearful in its beauty, a two-hundred meter high and fifty-meter wide <u>pillar</u> of water toward the sky.

"A full hit behind the second <u>funnel</u>!" I called down into the "Centrale." Then they cut loose down there for joy. They were carried away by <u>ecstasy</u> which <u>welled</u> out of their hearts, a joyous storm that ran through our entire boat and up to me.

And over there?

Landlubber, steel thy heart!

A terrible drama was being enacted on the hard-hit sinking ship. It listed and sank towards us. . . .

VOCABULARY
pillar—column that goes upward.
funnel—smokestack.
ecstasy—intense joy or delight.
welled—poured forth, rose up.

stop and write

Return to your K-W-L chart on page 42. In the **L** space, write the answers to your questions. The article may not answer all of them. Don't worry. You might have thought of other questions. Record them in the **W** space.

GATHER YOUR THOUGHTS

A. FIND A TOPIC Quick! Someone asks you, "What is this article about?" What do you say? The topic of the article is "what it's all about." Write a sentence that tells the topic of the selection.

"Adventures of the U-202" is about

_____

_____

B. LIST DETAILS List 4–5 important details about the topic that should be included in a summary of the writing. Keep them in the order they occur in the selection.

_____

_____

_____

_____

_____

_____

_____

_____

_____

_____

_____

A summary should
☞ include ideas in an order that makes sense, such as from the beginning to the end of the incident.
☞ use words like *first*, *next*, *finally*, and *then* to organize your thoughts.

IV. WRITE

Now use your list of details to write a **summary** of the selection. A summary tells what happens in the selection.
1. The first sentence should tell the topic and main idea. The other sentences should tell the important details.
2. Use the Writers' Checklist to help you revise.

(First sentence)

"Adventures of the U-202" tells Baron Spiegel's story about _____ .

(Summary)

WRITERS' CHECKLIST

CAPITALIZATION

❑ Did you capitalize the names of ships, but not words that are types of ships?
EXAMPLES: *the Centrale, steamer*

❑ Did you capitalize a person's title only if the title is used as part of a name?
EXAMPLES: *Captain Spiegel, Admiral Hall, the first mate, the crew*

❑ Did you capitalize the names of continents, countries, states, and bodies of water?
EXAMPLES: *Europe, Germany, Michigan, Atlantic Ocean*

❑ Did you capitalize the names of days of the week, months, and particular events in history?
EXAMPLES: *Tuesday, November, World War I*

V. WRAP-UP

What did you like best about the selection?

READERS' CHECKLIST

ENJOYMENT

❑ Did you like the reading?
❑ Was the reading experience pleasurable?
❑ Would you want to reread the piece or recommend it to someone?

Gwendolyn Brooks

Gwendolyn Brooks (1917–), an American writer and poet, grew up in Chicago. In 1950, she became the first African American to win a Pulitzer Prize. Her 1953 novel, *Maud Martha*, traces the growth of an African-American girl from the age of seven through adulthood.

Gwendolyn Brooks

Maud Martha

A NOVEL BY

Gwendolyn Brooks

Author of "A STREET IN BRONZEVILLE" and "ANNIE ALLEN" Pulitzer Prize winner

5: you're being so good, so kind

Did you ever look at a map before you started a trip? People do that to get an idea of what to expect. Good readers "walk through" the text before they begin reading. During a walk-through, you preview the story to come. This way, when you begin reading, the story feels more familiar.

BEFORE YOU READ
Read the title and opening paragraph of the story.
1. Thumb through the rest of the story.
2. Look for names and repeated words and notice the art. (These can give you clues about the selection's meaning.)
3. Make notes on a walk-through diagram on the next page.

"you're being so good, so kind" from *Maud Martha* by Gwendolyn Brooks

Maud Martha looked the living room over. Nicked old upright piano. Sag-seat leather armchair. Three or four straight chairs that had long ago given up the ghost of whatever shallow <u>dignity</u> they may have had in the beginning and looked completely disgusted with themselves and with the Brown family. Mantel with scroll decorations that usually seemed rather elegant but which since morning had become unspeakably <u>vulgar</u>, impossible.

VOCABULARY
dignity—honor or worthiness.
vulgar—common; of the great masses.

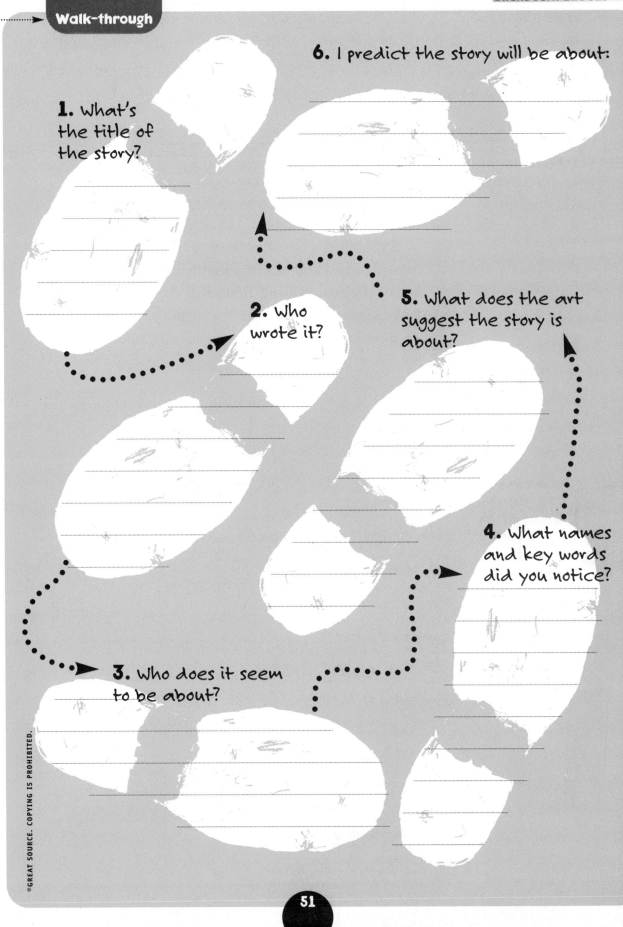

Walk-through

6. I predict the story will be about:

1. What's the title of the story?

2. Who wrote it?

5. What does the art suggest the story is about?

4. What names and key words did you notice?

3. Who does it seem to be about?

READ

Read the rest of Gwendolyn Brooks's story.

1. Write **questions** in the Response Notes about things you want to ask the author.
2. Write your thoughts about particular lines from the text in the double-entry journal spaces.

Response Notes

EXAMPLE:
How old is the
girl?

"you're being so good, so kind" continued

There was a small hole in the sad-colored rug, near the sofa. Not an outrageous hole. But she <u>shuddered</u>. She dashed to the sofa, <u>maneuvered</u> it till the hole could not be seen.

She sniffed a couple of times. Often it was said that colored people's houses necessarily had a certain heavy, unpleasant smell. Nonsense, that was. Vicious—and nonsense. But she raised every window.

Here was the theory of racial equality about to be put into practice, and she only hoped she would be equal to being equal.

No matter how <u>taut</u> the terror, the fall proceeds to its <u>dregs</u>. . . .

Double-Entry Journal

Quotation	My response (my thoughts and feelings)
"Here was the theory of racial equality about to be put into practice, and she only hoped she would be equal to being equal."	

VOCABULARY
shuddered—shivered out of fear.
maneuvered—shifted.
taut—pulled or drawn tight with fear.
dregs—most worthless parts; left-over parts.

At seven o'clock her heart was starting to make itself heard, and with great energy she was assuring herself that, though she liked Charles, though she admired Charles, it was only at the high school that she wanted to see Charles.

This was no Willie or Richard or Sylvester coming to call on her. Neither was she Charles's Sally or Joan. She was the whole "colored" race, and Charles was the personalization of the entire Caucasian plan.

Double-Entry Journal

Quotation	My response (my thoughts and feelings)
"She was the whole 'colored' race, and Charles was the personalization of the entire Caucasian plan."	

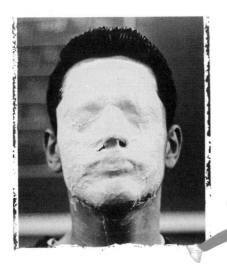

VOCABULARY
personalization—model or example.
Caucasian—white person.

At three minutes to eight the bell rang, hesitantly. Charles! No doubt regretting his <u>impulse</u> already. No doubt regarding, with a <u>rueful</u> <u>contempt</u>, the outside of the house, so badly in need of paint. Those <u>rickety</u> steps. She retired into the bathroom. Presently she heard her father go to the door; her father—walking slowly, walking patiently, walking unafraid, as if about to let in a paper boy who wanted his twenty cents, or an insurance man, or Aunt Vivian, or no more than Woodette Williams, her own silly friend.

What was this she was feeling now? Not fear, not fear. A sort of gratitude! It sickened her to realize it. As though Charles, in coming, gave her a gift.

<u>Recipient</u> and <u>benefactor</u>.

It's so good of you.

You're being so good.

VOCABULARY
impulse—motivating force.
rueful—sad; regretful.
contempt—open disrespect; disdain.
rickety—likely to break or fall apart.
recipient—one who receives.
benefactor—one who gives aid or benefits.

Double-Entry Journal

Quotation	My response (my thoughts and feelings)
"As though Charles, in coming, gave her a gift."	

GATHER YOUR THOUGHTS

A. UNDERSTAND CHARACTERS Make notes about Maud Martha. Who is she? What is she like? In each of the circles surrounding her name, write a word that describes her.

CREATING CHARACTER CLUSTERS

- Put the character's name in the center.
- Use some of the outside circles for what you know about the character.
- Use the other circles for what you have inferred—that is, the guesses you've made about the character.

Maud Martha

nervous

B. DESCRIBE A CHARACTER Write at least 2 things that Maud Martha is like and 2 things she is not like.

1. Maud Martha is like

2. She is also like

3. Maud Martha is not like

4. She is also not like

IV. WRITE

Now write a **descriptive paragraph** about Maud Martha.

1. Begin with a topic sentence that makes a general statement about her.
2. Use details to help your readers really "see" this character.
3. Use the Writers' Checklist to help you revise.

V. WRAP-UP

What are some of the things that "you're being so good, so kind" made you think about?

Who can resist the excitement and bright lights of the big city? Think about that question as you read the next story. But reading is more than just taking in words on a page. Reading also involves listening and reacting to what you read.

BEFORE YOU READ

Choose a reader who will read with expression.
1. Have the reader read the story's title and opening paragraphs.
2. Listen carefully.
3. Then complete the Listener's Guide below.

"Maud Martha and New York" from *Maud Martha* by Gwendolyn Brooks

The name "New York" glittered in front of her like the silver in the shops on Michigan Boulevard. It was silver, and it was solid, and it was <u>remote</u>: it was behind glass, it was behind bright glass like the silver in the shops. It was not for her. Yet.

When she was out walking, and with <u>grating</u> iron swish a train whipped by, off, above, its passengers were always, for her comfort, New York-bound. She sat inside with them. She leaned back in the <u>plush</u>. She sped, past farms, through tiny towns, where people slept, kissed, quarreled, ate midnight snacks; unfortunate folk who were not New York-bound and never would be.

VOCABULARY
remote—located far away; distant.
grating—making a harsh grinding sound because of things rubbing together.
plush—soft, thick fabric, as of silk, that has a thick, deep pile.

My Listener's Guide   SELECTION TITLE:_____

AUTHOR:_____

WORDS OR PHRASES THAT CAUGHT MY ATTENTION:

I PREDICT THIS STORY WILL BE INTERESTING / DULL. (CIRCLE ONE)

I THINK THIS STORY WILL BE EASY / HARD TO UNDERSTAND. (CIRCLE ONE)

I'D RATHER BE A LISTENER / READER. (CIRCLE ONE)

With a partner or group, finish reading Brooks's story.
1. Have several different readers take turns.
2. As you listen, **react** to the place that Maud Martha describes. Try to **visualize** what what she sees by making sketches in the Response Notes.

Response Notes

EXAMPLE:
Sounds like a mansion!

"Maud Martha and New York" continued

Maud Martha loved it when her magazines said "New York," described "good" objects there, wonderful people there, recalled fine talk, the <u>bristling</u> or the creamy or the <u>tactfully</u> <u>shimmering</u> ways of life. They showed pictures of rooms with wood paneling, softly glowing, touched up by the compliment of a spot of <u>auburn</u> here, the low burn of a rare binding there. There were <u>ferns</u> in these rooms, and Chinese boxes; bits of dreamlike crystal; a taste of leather. In the advertisement pages, you saw where you could buy six Italian plates for eleven hundred dollars—and you must hurry, for there was just the one set; you saw where you could buy <u>antique</u> French <u>bisque</u> <u>figurines</u> (pale blue and gold) for—for— Her whole body become a hunger, she would <u>pore</u> over these pages. The clothes interested her, too; especially did she care for the pictures of women wearing carelessly, as if they were rags, dresses that were plain but whose prices were not. And the foolish food (her mother's description) enjoyed by New Yorkers fascinated her. They paid ten dollars for an eight-ounce jar of Russian <u>caviar</u>; they

VOCABULARY
bristling—ruffling or disturbing.
tactfully—with sensitivity to what is proper or appropriate.
shimmering—appearing as a wavering or flickering image.
auburn—reddish brown to brown color.
ferns—flowerless green plants used often for decoration.
antique—typical of an earlier period.
bisque—unglazed ceramic.
figurines—small molded or sculptured figures.
pore—read or study attentively.
caviar—eggs of a large fish, eaten as a delicacy.

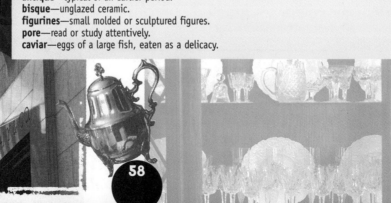

ate things called <u>anchovies</u>, and <u>capers</u>; they ate little diamond-shaped cheeses that paprika had but breathed on; they ate bitter-almond <u>macaroons</u>; they ate papaya packed in rum and syrup; they ate peculiar sauces, were free with honey, were lavish with butter, wine and cream.

stop+think

What does Maud Martha like most about New York?

Sketch some of her favorite things here.

stop+think

She bought the New York papers downtown, read of the concerts and plays, studied the book reviews, was intent over the announcements of <u>auctions</u>. She liked the sound of "Fifth Avenue, "Town Hall," "<u>B. Altman</u>," "<u>Hammacher Schlemmer</u>." She was on Fifth Avenue whenever she wanted to be, and she it was who rolled up, silky or furry, in the taxi, was assisted out, and stood, her next step <u>nebulous</u>, before the theaters of the thousand lights, before velvet-lined impossible shops; she it was.

VOCABULARY

anchovies—small, herring-like fish used in cooking.
capers—pickled flower buds used to add flavor to food.
macaroons—chewy cookies.
auctions—public sales in which property or goods are sold to the highest bidder.
B. Altman, Hammacher Schlemmer—fancy, upscale department stores.
nebulous—cloudy, misty, or hazy.

New York, for Maud Martha, was a symbol. Her idea of it stood for what she felt life ought to be. Jeweled. Polished. Smiling. Poised. Calmly rushing! Straight up and down, yet graceful enough.

She thought of them drinking their coffee there—or tea, as in England. It was afternoon. <u>Lustrous</u> people glided over perfect floors, correctly smiling. They stopped before a drum table, covered with heavy white—and bearing a silver coffee service, old (in the better sense) china, a platter of orange and cinnamon cakes (or was it nutmeg the cakes would have in them?), sugar and cream, a Chinese box, one tall and slender flower. Their host or hostess poured, smiling too, nodding quickly to this one and that one, inquiring gently whether it should be sugar, or cream, or both, or neither. (She was teaching herself to drink coffee with neither.) All was very gentle. The voices, no matter how they rose, or even sharpened, had fur at the base. The steps never bragged, or <u>grated</u> in any way on any ear—not that they could very well, on so good a Persian rug, or deep soft carpeting. And the drum table stood in front of a screen, a Japanese one, perhaps, with rich and mellow, bread-textured colors. The people drank and nibbled, while they discussed the issues of the day, sorting, rejecting, revising. Then they went home, quietly, elegantly. They retired to homes

VOCABULARY
Lustrous—gleaming with brilliant light.
grated—scraped; irritated.

"Maud Martha and New York" continued

not one <u>whit</u> less solid or <u>embroidered</u> than the home of their host or hostess.

What she wanted to dream, and dreamed, was her affair. It pleased her to dwell upon color and soft <u>bready</u> textures and light, on a complex beauty, on gemlike surfaces. What was the matter with that? Besides, who could safely swear that she would never be able to make her dream come true for herself? Not altogether, then!—but slightly?—in some part?

She was eighteen years old, and the world waited. To <u>caress</u> her.

▌VOCABULARY

whit—bit.
embroidered—decorated with fancy details.
bready—like bread.
caress—treat fondly or favorably; cherish.

FINISH THESE SENTENCES.

1. For Maud Martha, New York means

2. Maud Martha wants to be

3. She doesn't want to be

WRITE 6 OR MORE ADJECTIVES (DESCRIPTIVE WORDS) ABOUT MAUD MARTHA AND NEW YORK.

1.   4.

2.   5.

3.   6.

GATHER YOUR THOUGHTS

A. SKETCH Brooks uses vivid description to paint a picture with words.

1. Review the notes and sketches you made while listening to the story.

2. Then draw a picture of the New York that Maud Martha has shown you.

B. BRAINSTORM DETAILS Create a word web below to brainstorm details to describe a place important to you.

1. Write the place in the center of the word web.

2. Then add as many descriptive words as you can.

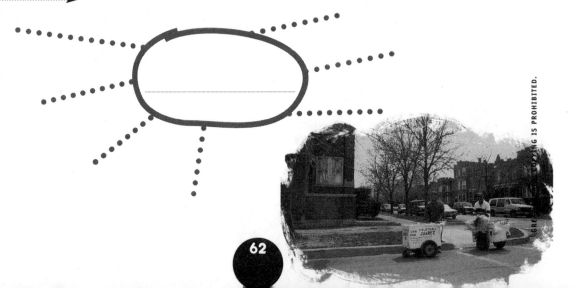

WRITE

Now write a **descriptive paragraph** about a place that is important to you.

1. Use a lot of description, just as Gwendolyn Brooks does in "Maud Martha and New York," so that readers can visualize the place that you describe.

2. Use the Writers' Checklist to help you revise your paragraph.

(title) ◄ ....

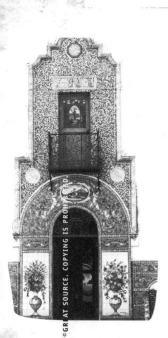

Continue writing on the next page.

WRITERS' CHECKLIST

COMMA SPLICES

☐ Did you avoid comma splices? A comma splice occurs when two simple sentences are joined with just a comma.
EXAMPLE: The city is beautiful, I love it.
To correct a comma splice, insert a comma plus a joining word (and, or, but) or a semicolon (;) between the two sentences.
Another option to fix the comma splice is to create two different sentences.
EXAMPLE: The city is beautiful, and I love it.

Continue your writing from the previous page.

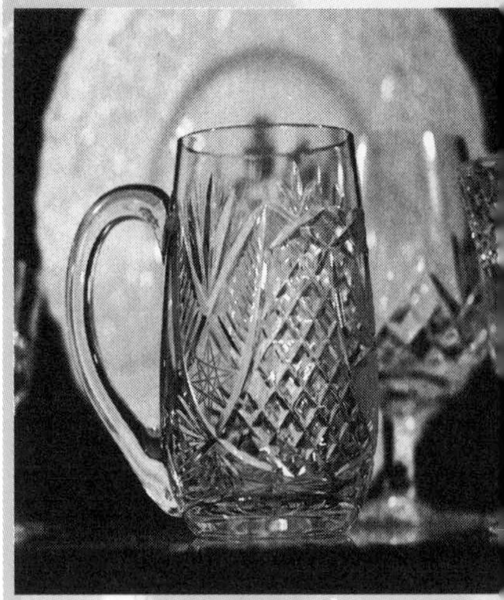

V. WRAP-UP

Is the story "Maud Martha in New York" well written? Why or why not?

READERS' CHECKLIST

STYLE

- ❑ Did you find the passage well written?
- ❑ Are the sentences well constructed and the words well chosen?
- ❑ Does the style show you how to be a better writer?

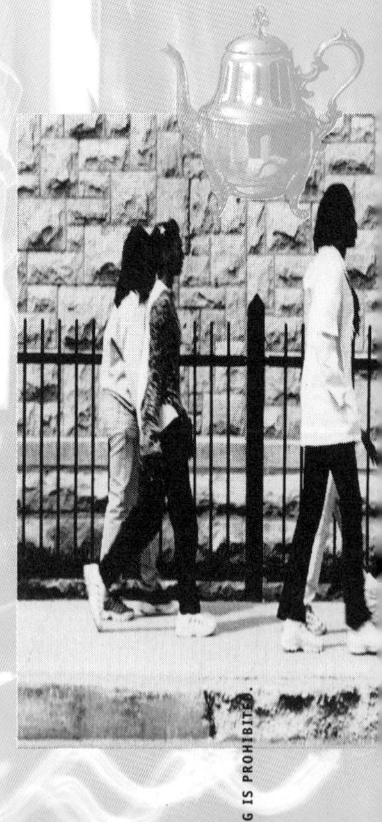

New Lands

Themes of being alone, in unfamiliar lands, are common in literature. Literature lets us hear "new voices" different from our own.

immigrant n. a person who has recently appeared for the first time in a place; an alien.

Is a picture worth a thousand words? Who knows the exact number, but pictures can sometimes make ideas easier to understand. Before you read, look for pictures to help you understand the subject. They can help you predict what a story or article might be about and help you understand what you are reading.

BEFORE YOU READ

Walk through the pictures in this lesson.
1. Look at each of the pictures.
2. Ask yourself: How do these pictures make me feel?

3. Stop a moment and think. Based on the pictures, what are these poems probably about?

II. READ

Read the two poems.
1. Think about how the poems make you feel. What do they make you think about?
2. **React** to them and jot down your ideas as you read. Connect what's being described to your own feelings and experiences.

"Legal Alien" by Pat Mora

Bi-lingual, Bi-cultural,
able to slip from "How's life?"
to *"Me'stan volviendo loca,"*
able to sit in a paneled office
drafting memos in smooth English,
able to order in fluent Spanish
at a Mexican restaurant,
American but hyphenated,
viewed by Anglos as perhaps <u>exotic</u>,
perhaps inferior, definitely different,
viewed by Mexicans as alien,
(their eyes say, "You may speak
Spanish but you're not like me")
an American to Mexicans
a Mexican to Americans
a handy token
sliding back and forth
between the <u>fringes</u> of both worlds,
by smiling
by masking the discomfort
of being pre-judged
<u>Bi-laterally</u>.

RESPONSE NOTES

EXAMPLE:
It must be hard to feel like you don't fit in.

VOCABULARY
exotic—strangely beautiful.
fringes—outer edges.
Bi-laterally—having or involving two sides.

LA MANO

A double-entry journal can help you gather your thoughts about a poem.

1. On one side of the journal, write lines from the poem. The lines you select may be ones you like or ones that make you think about something.

2. In the other column, write your thoughts and feelings about the lines.

DOUBLE-ENTRY JOURNAL

QUOTES	MY THOUGHTS
EXAMPLE: "American but hyphenated"	"Hyphenated" means having two different names or labels. The speaker must feel caught between two groups, not a part of either one.
1.	
2.	
3.	

"Immigrants" by Pat Mora

wrap their babies in the American flag,
feed them mashed hot dogs and apple pie,
name them Bill and Daisy,
buy them blonde dolls that blink blue
eyes or a football and tiny cleats
before the baby can even walk,
speak to them in thick English,
hallo, babee, hallo,
whisper in Spanish or Polish
when the babies sleep, whisper
in a dark parent bed, that dark
parent fear, "Will they like
our boy, our girl, our fine american
boy, our fine american girl?"

TIPS FOR RESPONDING TO POEMS

- Write your own thoughts and reactions instead of just retelling the author's words.
- Think about how the lines make you feel or what they teach you.
- Share your ideas with a friend. Explain why the lines make you feel a certain way.

Use the double-entry journal to react to the poem. Choose lines or phrases to put in the left column and write your reactions to them in the right column.

DOUBLE-ENTRY JOURNAL

QUOTES	MY THOUGHTS
EXAMPLE: "buy them blonde dolls that blink blue"	He means dolls have only one skin color—white, with blue eyes.
1.	
2.	
3.	

GATHER YOUR THOUGHTS

A. BRAINSTORM Both of the poems describe what it is like to be in a new land. Choose one of the poems and create a web.

1. In the center of the web, write a word or two that tell how the speaker feels about being in a new land.

2. Draw lines from the center of the web.

3. On the lines, write words or images from the poem that show you how the speaker feels.

B. REMEMBER AN EXPERIENCE Now think of a time when you were in a new place. Maybe you weren't in a new land, but you were in a new neighborhood or school, you joined a new club, or you just felt alone and on the outside.

1. Create a web to gather your thoughts about the experience.

2. In the middle of the web, write how you felt.

3. On lines from the web, write ideas, images, and words that come to mind when you think about the experience.

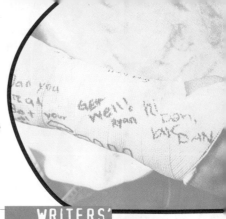

IV. WRITE

You have just read two poems about being in a new land. Now write your own **poem** about being somewhere new.

1. Return to your web. Circle words and ideas that you think would work well in your poem.
2. Model your poem on "Immigrants." The title could sum up the experience—such as "New School" or "First Day."
3. Use the Writers' Checklist to help you revise.

V. WRAP-UP

What did reading the two poems make you think about?

You look outside and notice that the sky is getting dark, even though it is only noon. The branches on the trees are bending in the wind. You go around your house, closing all the open windows. Why do you close the windows? Because you anticipate—you <u>expect</u>—rain to fall. When you read, you can also anticipate. When you find out a little about a story or an article, you can anticipate what might be ahead.

BEFORE YOU READ

Complete the Anticipation Guide.

1. Rank each statement from 1 to 10 according to how much you agree or disagree with it.

Boys do better at mathematics than girls.
1 2 3 4 5 6 7 8 9 10
(STRONGLY DISAGREE)　　　　　　　　(STRONGLY AGREE)

Being accepted by peers is more important than success in school.
1 2 3 4 5 6 7 8 9 10
(STRONGLY DISAGREE)　　　　　　　　(STRONGLY AGREE)

Cultural differences can cause confusion and embarrassment.
1 2 3 4 5 6 7 8 9 10
(STRONGLY DISAGREE)　　　　　　　　(STRONGLY AGREE)

Mathematics is a difficult subject for boys and girls.
1 2 3 4 5 6 7 8 9 10
(STRONGLY DISAGREE)　　　　　　　　(STRONGLY AGREE)

I think "Who's Hu?" will be about

2. Discuss your responses in a small group. Talk about why you ranked each statement as you did.

3. Based on these statements, make a prediction.

....

....

....

....

ANTICIPATION GUIDE

READ

Read the story.
1. As you read, underline the main events that happen.
2. **Clarify** what's happening by listing the main events in the Response Notes.

RESPONSE NOTES

EXAMPLE:

1. corrects others in her math class

"A Simple Proposition" from *Who's Hu?*
by Lensey Namioka

I was tired of being a <u>freak</u>.

My father was a professor of mathematics at <u>M.I.T.</u>, and whenever I got 100 on my math test (which was pretty often) my high school teachers would say, "I know where Emma Hu gets help with her homework . . . <u>cackle</u> . . . cackle. . . ." The rest of the class usually cackled along. At first I didn't see why they were so nasty about it. Later I discovered that girls in this country weren't supposed to be good in math. The teachers didn't like it when Arthur Aldrich—our self-styled math genius—corrected their mistakes in class. They hated it a lot more when I did.

In China there was nothing wrong with girls being good at math. In fact, Chinese women were supposed to keep the household or business accounts. But in America, when I opened my big mouth to correct my algebra teacher—in broken English, yet—everyone thought I was a freak. Once I thought I would cheat on my math test by deliberately making a couple of mistakes, but when it came to the point, I just couldn't do it. Mathematics was too beautiful to mess up.

On most days I wasn't too bothered by my math grades, but lately I had begun to worry. I was a senior at Evesham High, a high school in the suburbs of Boston, and the senior prom was only three weeks away. Who was going to ask a Chinese girl math whiz? According to my friend Katey, everybody went to the prom except the freaks.

VOCABULARY
freak—person, thing, or event that is highly unusual or irregular.
M.I.T.—Massachusetts Institute of Technology.
cackle—laugh in a shrill manner.

Katey was blonde, pretty, and tall. She had been booked for the prom since her junior year, ever since she began going steady with her current boy friend. I was just over five feet, and when we walked to our classes together, we looked like Mutt and Jeff.

She was even more anxious than I was to see me at the prom. At lunchtime she kept pressing me. "Emma, all the rest of us are going, and it won't be fun if you're not there!"

There were murmurs of agreement from the rest of our set at the lunch table. I sat silent, too choked to speak. These were genuine friends, and they were sorry at the thought that I might be left out. I couldn't allow myself to be classified with the freaks and the weirdos who never went to anything.

Fill out the graphic organizer.

SETTING
where and when the story takes place

PROBLEM
problem that a character needs to solve

GOAL
what the character wants to happen

After lunch the first class I attended was math. Just being in the classroom made me feel better. I liked to look around the room at the portion of the blackboard painted with a permanent white grid for graphing

VOCABULARY
permanent—lasting or remaining without essential change; unchanging.

equations, the hanging cardboard models of regular polyhedra we had made as a class project, and the oak shelf containing plaster models of conic sections and various surfaces. My favorite was the hyperbolic paraboloid, or saddle, with its straight lines neatly incised in the plaster.

The class was Advanced Mathematics, intended for seniors who were going into science or math and who had already taken algebra, geometry, and trig. The course covered analytic geometry, calculus, and a little probability theory. Actually, it wasn't so much the content of the course that I liked best: it was the teacher, Mr. Antonelli. He was a short man only a little taller than I, and he had a swarthy face dominated by a huge beak of a nose. Unlike my other math teachers (one of them even a woman), he didn't seem to find it bizarre that a girl should do well in his class. As for my being Chinese, I doubt if he even noticed. Mr. Antonelli didn't care if you were a Martian eunuch, as long as you did the math correctly.

Today Mr. Antonelli gave the impression of suppressed excitement. He clearly had something on his mind, because for the first time I remember, he let one of the boys do a maximum-minimum problem without checking the second derivative to see if it was an inflection point. Arthur Aldrich and I beat each other to a draw in pointing out the mistake. Mr. Antonelli acknowledged our reproof almost absentmindedly. He certainly was preoccupied.

With five minutes left of the period, Mr. Antonelli made an announcement: "Class, you remember that

VOCABULARY
polythedra—solids formed by geometric planes.
hyperbolic paraboloid—complex mathematical figure or shape.
incised—cut.
Martian eunuch—weirdo from Mars.
derivative—complicated math term.
inflection point—point where a curve changes shape.
reproof—act of scolding or correcting.

last fall you all took the semi-final exam for the Sterns Mathematics Prize. Today I received word of the results."

The Sterns was a mathematics prize given annually to a high school senior in Massachusetts. The award was for $200, but the prestige it carried was immeasurable. Never in the history of the Sterns Prize had it been won by a girl.

"Now," Mr. Antonelli went on, "it is an honor for our school if a student here makes it to the finals. Well, we've got not just one student, but two who are going into the finals. One is Arthur Aldrich."

Arthur was a tall, gangly boy with hair so blond that it looked almost white. With his long nose and sharp chin, he reminded me of a white fox in one of the Chinese fairy tales. Arthur had very few stumbling blocks in his life. His family was comfortably off, he did well in every subject in school, and he was a credit to the Evesham High School track team. In spite of his successes, Arthur was too <u>arrogant</u> to be popular.

"The other," Mr. Antonelli announced, "is Emma Hu."

PLOT CHART

List in order 3 things that have happened so far.

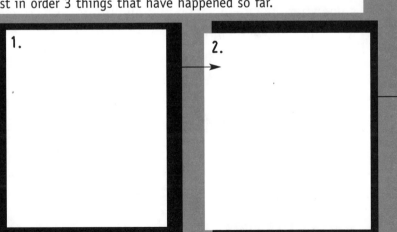

1.

2.

3.

VOCABULARY
arrogant—too proud; thinking too much of one's self.

The class cheered. My thoughts were in a whirl. I thought I had fallen down badly on the exam the previous fall because there were two problems I hadn't been able to do. Now it seemed that my performance hadn't been so bad after all.

I have only the vaguest memories of my other classes that afternoon. I barely realized when the final bell rang. Leaving school, I almost hugged my books to my chest. It was like waking up on my birthday and finding a pile of presents outside my door.

My mother probably felt like this when she looked over a new piece of music, and my father when he received a new set of Chinese pulp novels.

I was so absorbed that I didn't hear footsteps coming up behind me. I jumped when Arthur's voice spoke in my ear. "I want to talk to you."

"About what?" I asked, surprised. To my knowledge he had never asked any girl to anything before. In Arthur's ranking of animal intelligence, girls came somewhere between sheep and myna birds. Of course that made me even more of a freak in his eyes.

Arthur and I must have made a strange-looking pair. His ash-blond hair curled around his thin foxy face, while my long hair, blue-black and straight as a <u>linear function</u>, framed my heart-shaped face. Not only did we belong to different races, we hardly belonged to the same species. The only thing we had in common was mathematics.

VOCABULARY

linear function—math term having to do with lines.

When he had seen that I threatened to become a rival, Arthur began a systematic campaign to discourage me. In this he had the support of our previous math teachers. They kept hinting that for a girl to do well in math was unfeminine, unnatural, and unattractive.

At first I hadn't been too bothered. My English had been shaky, and subtle hints were lost on me. Anyway, being teased about my math had been submerged in the larger misery of being an alien. But by my junior year at Evesham, I began to be really uncomfortable. In my trig class I made a lot of mistakes in looking up trigonometric functions, and my math grades slid. My parents were disturbed but couldn't think of a reason. It was my older brother, Emerson, who had looked over my homework papers and found my mistakes. He insisted on having my eyes checked, and when I turned out to have 20-20 vision, he gave me a stern lecture and told me to shape up. My grades went back up.

In our Advanced Mathematics class, Arthur had found no support from the teacher, Mr. Antonelli. Although Mr. Antonelli was a wonderful teacher, his manner was dry and impersonal. He kept personalities out of the classroom entirely.

By using our last names, he made me forget I was the only girl in a class with eight boys. He also made all of us feel very adult.

Arthur grinned now. In the illustrations of my Chinese fairy tale book, foxes grinned with their mouths forming a big V. Arthur's smile was just like that. "I hear you want to go to the senior prom but can't find anyone to take you. I have a simple <u>proposition</u> to make: I'll take you to the prom—refreshments, <u>corsage</u>, dinner afterward, the whole works—if you'll drop out of the Sterns exam."

CHARACTER DEVELOPMENT

Note how the characters have changed in the story.

	at the beginning	at the end
EMMA		
ARTHUR		

The sheer <u>gall</u> of his proposition took my breath away, and for a moment I was too astounded even to be angry. In the end my main reaction turned out to be triumph. "So you're really afraid I might do better than you on the exam!" I said, unable to hide my satisfaction.

Two spots of color appeared on Arthur's pale cheeks, but he kept his foxy grin. "I can do better than you any day, don't you worry! But I know you're desperate to go to the prom. Every red-blooded, normal high school senior goes to the prom, right?"

I said nothing. The price of being a red-blooded, normal high school senior was pretty high.

"Well?" demanded Arthur.

I was determined to be equally curt. "No," I said.

At that, Arthur's normally deep voice went up.

VOCABULARY
proposition—offer.
corsage—small bouquet of flowers worn by a woman.
gall—nerve.

"A Simple Proposition" continued

"What do you mean, no? You've decided to give up the prom?"

"Arthur, if I accepted your offer just to be able to go to the prom, I'd always be ashamed of myself."

There were some sputters as Arthur finally convinced himself I really meant what I said. "This is your last chance, Emma. Nobody else in the whole school would dream of asking you."

"There are more important things than the prom, Arthur."

"Now you're sounding high and mighty, aren't you?" Arthur sneered. "Don't give me that, Emma. Everybody in school knows you're dying to go."

"It's true, I was dying to go to the prom," I said wearily. "But I've changed my mind."

Fill out the graphic organizer.

CLIMAX
high point
or
turning
point
of
story

RESOLUTION
what happens with the character's goal

VOCABULARY
sputters—short bursts of spitting and popping sounds.

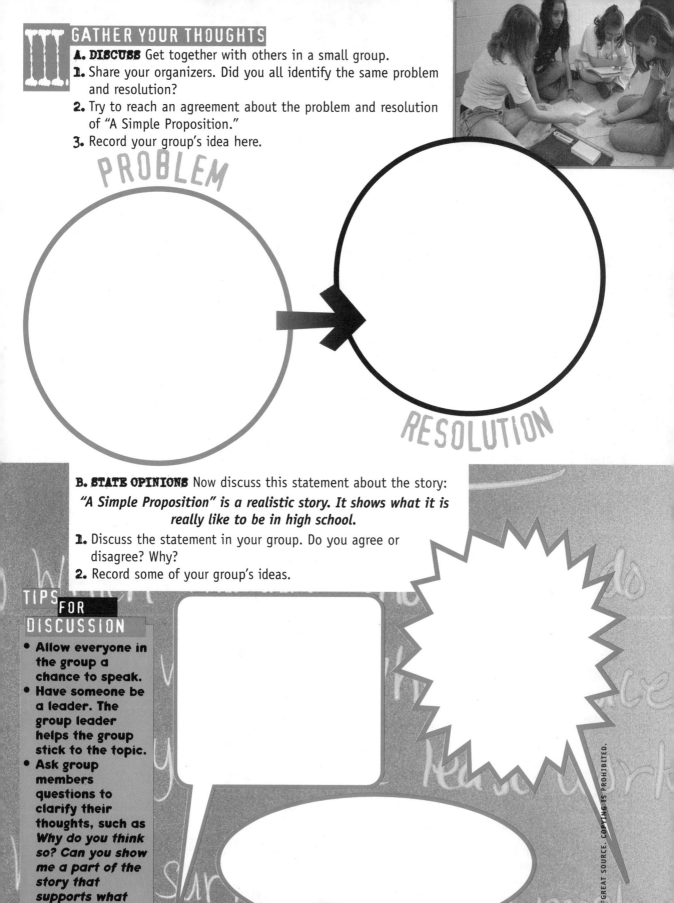

III GATHER YOUR THOUGHTS

A. DISCUSS Get together with others in a small group.

1. Share your organizers. Did you all identify the same problem and resolution?
2. Try to reach an agreement about the problem and resolution of "A Simple Proposition."
3. Record your group's idea here.

PROBLEM

RESOLUTION

B. STATE OPINIONS Now discuss this statement about the story:

"A Simple Proposition" is a realistic story. It shows what it is really like to be in high school.

1. Discuss the statement in your group. Do you agree or disagree? Why?
2. Record some of your group's ideas.

TIPS FOR DISCUSSION

- **Allow everyone in the group a chance to speak.**
- **Have someone be a leader. The group leader helps the group stick to the topic.**
- **Ask group members questions to clarify their thoughts, such as *Why do you think so? Can you show me a part of the story that supports what you are saying?***

C. FORM YOUR OPINIONS Imagine that you are writing a review of "A Simple Proposition" for your school newspaper. The review needs to answer these questions:

1. Is "A Simple Proposition" a realistic story?
Yes or No   For these reasons:

2. Is "A Simple Proposition" a story that you would recommend to your classmates?   Yes or No   For these reasons:

IV. WRITE

Write a **review** of "A Simple Proposition" for your school newspaper.
1. Start your review with a topic sentence that gives your opinion and recommendation about the story.
2. In the rest of the review, support your opinion with ideas from the story and from your own experiences.
3. Use the Writers' Checklist to help you revise.

EXAMPLE: TOPIC SENTENCE

"A Simple Proposition" is only partly realistic, but I would recommend it because it is interesting and makes readers think about how they should treat other people.

WRITERS' CHECKLIST

CAPITALIZATION
❑ Did you capitalize the names of cities and states?
EXAMPLES: *Austin, Texas; Seattle, Washington*
❑ Did you capitalize the name of a school, but not the word school unless it is part of the school's name?
EXAMPLE: *Our high school is Aurora West High School.*

Continue your writing on the next page.

Continue your writing from the previous page.

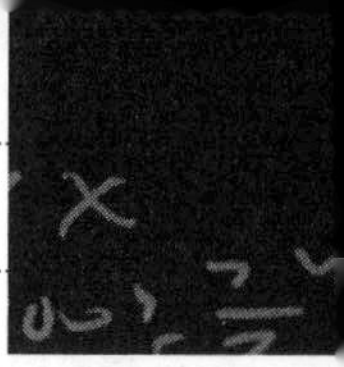

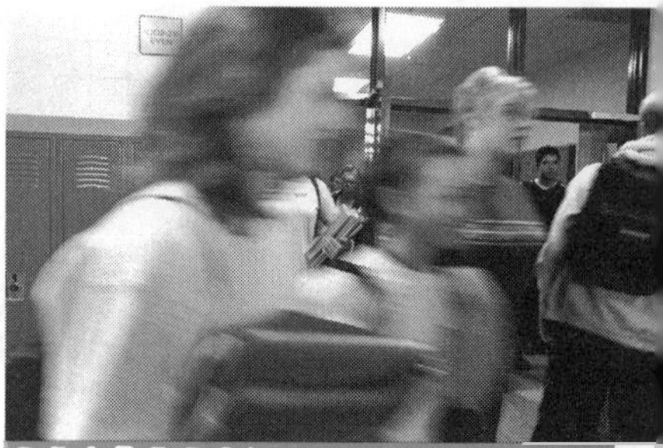

V. WRAP-UP

Imagine that you met the author of "A Simple Proposition" and asked her what point she was trying to make when she wrote this story. What would she say?

READERS' CHECKLIST

UNDERSTANDING

- ❑ Did you understand the reading?
- ❑ Was the message or point clear?
- ❑ Can you restate what the reading is about?

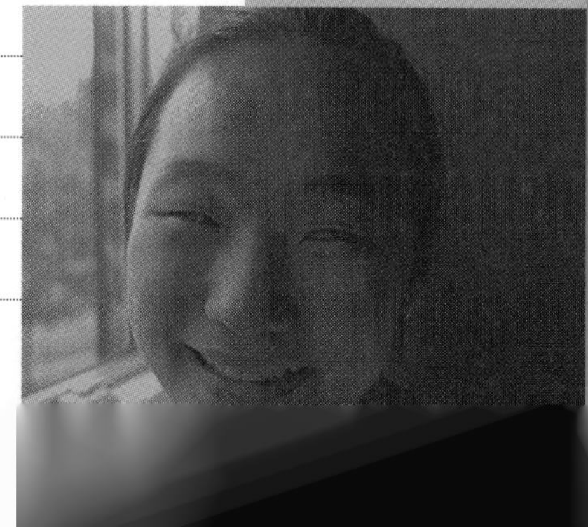

Cyclops

Cerberus, the
three-headed dog

Myths and Monsters

Mythology tells stories about larger-than-life
figures—fierce monsters and great heroes.

Hercules

Do you like stories about monsters? Then you'll love the action-packed stories of famous myths. A story's plot is its action. Good readers know to keep track of a story's plot as they read.

BEFORE YOU READ

Preview the selection by reading the title and the first paragraph.
1. Answer the questions on the Preview Card.
2. Get together with a partner and share cards:
3. Discuss similarities and differences in your guesses about the plot.

"The Cyclops' Cave" by Bernard Evslin

Ulysses had no way of knowing it, but in the entire sea this was the very worst island on which the small party could have landed. For here lived the Cyclopes, huge <u>savage</u> creatures, tall as trees, each with one eye in the middle of his forehead. Once long ago, they had lived in the <u>bowels</u> of Olympus, forging thunderbolts for Zeus. But he had punished them for some fault, exiling them to this island where they had forgotten all their <u>smithcraft</u> and did nothing but fight with each other for the herds of wild goats, to find enough food to fill their huge bellies. Best of all, they liked storms; storms meant shipwrecks. Shipwrecks meant sailors struggling in the sea, who could be plucked out and eaten raw; and the thing they loved best in the world was human flesh. The largest and the fiercest and the hungriest of all the Cyclopes was one named Polyphemus. He kept constant <u>vigil</u> on his mountain, in fair weather or foul. If he spotted a ship, and there was no storm to help, he would dive into the sea and swim underwater, coming up underneath the ship and overturning it. Then he would swim off with his pockets full of sailors.

VOCABULARY
savage—wild.
bowels—insides of something.
smithcraft—making of small metal objects.
vigil—watch.

Preview Card

Answer these questions. If you don't know an answer, just make a guess.

WHO ARE THE CYCLOPES?

WHY MIGHT ULYSSES FEEL SORRY FOR THE CYCLOPES?

HOW WILL THE CYCLOPES FEEL ABOUT ULYSSES COMING ONTO THEIR ISLAND?

WHAT DO YOU THINK THE PLOT WILL BE ABOUT?

READ

Read the rest of this excerpt from "The Cyclops' Cave."

1. Find at least 4 important things that happen in the story. **Clarify** them in your mind by writing 1, 2, 3, 4, and so on in the Response Notes.

2. Also jot down predictions about what will happen next.

"The Cyclops' Cave" continued

On this day, he could not believe his luck when he saw a boat actually landing on the beach and thirteen meaty-looking sailors <u>disembark</u> and begin to march toward his cave. But there they were, climbing out of the valley now, up the slope of the hill, right toward the cave. He realized they must be hunting his goats.

The door of the cave was an enormous slab of stone. He shoved this aside so that the cave stood invitingly open, casting a faint glow of firelight upon the dusk. Over the fire, on a great spit, eight goats were turning and roasting. The delicious <u>savors</u> of the cooking drifted from the cave. Polyphemus lay down behind a huge boulder and waited.

The men were halfway up the slope of the hill when they smelled the meat roasting. They broke into a run. Ulysses tried to <u>restrain</u> them, but they paid no <u>heed</u>—they were too hungry. They raced to the mouth of the

VOCABULARY
disembark—go ashore from a ship.
savors—tastes or smells.
restrain—hold back or keep in check.
heed—notice; attention.

Response Notes

EXAMPLE:
1. Polyphemus sees Ulysses's boat land on island.

cave and dashed in. Ulysses drew his sword and hurried after them. When he saw the huge fireplace and the eight goats spitted like sparrows, his heart sank because he knew that they had come into reach of something much larger than themselves. However, the men were giving no thought to anything but food; they flung themselves on the spit and tore into the goat meat, smearing their hands and faces with sizzling fat, too hungry to feel pain as they crammed the hot meat into their mouths.

stop + predict

What will happen when Polyphemus sees the men eating his goats?

stop + predict

There was a loud rumbling sound; the cave darkened. Ulysses whirled around. He saw that the door had been closed. The far end of the cavern was too dark to see anything, but then—amazed, aghast— he saw what looked like a huge red lantern far above, coming closer. Then he saw the great shadow of a nose under it and the gleam of teeth. He realized that the lantern was a great flaming eye. Then he saw the whole giant, tall as a tree, with huge fingers reaching out of the shadows, fingers bigger than baling hooks. They closed around two sailors and hauled them screaming into the air.

As Ulysses and his horrified men watched, the great hand bore the struggling little men to the giant's mouth. He ate them, still wriggling, the way a cat eats a grasshopper; he ate them clothes and all, growling over their raw bones.

VOCABULARY

spitted—stuck on a metal bar and roasted over a fire.
aghast—struck by shock, terror, or amazement.
baling hooks—large, curved pieces of metal used for lifting hay.

"The Cyclops' Cave" continued

The men had fallen to their knees and were whimpering like terrified children, but Ulysses stood there, sword in hand, his agile brain working more swiftly than it ever had before.

"Greetings," he called. "May I know to whom we are indebted for such hospitality?"

The giant belched and spat out buttons. "I am Polyphemus," he growled. "This is my cave, my mountain, and everything that comes here is mine. I do hope you can all stay to dinner. There are just enough of you to make a meal. Ho, ho . . . " And he laughed a great, choking, phlegmy laugh, swiftly lunged, and caught another sailor, whom he lifted into the air and held before his face.

"Wait!" cried Ulysses.

"What for?"

"You won't enjoy him that way. He is from Attica, where the olives grow. He was raised on olives and has a very delicate, oily flavor. But to appreciate it, you must taste the wine of the country."

"Wine? What is wine?"

"It is a drink. Made from pressed grapes. Have you never drunk it?"

"We drink nothing but ox blood and buttermilk here."

"Ah, you do not know what you have missed, gentle Polyphemus. Meat-eaters, in particular, love wine. Here, try it for yourself."

stop + predict

What plan do you think Ulysses has in mind?

_____

_____

_____

VOCABULARY
whimpering—crying, sobbing, or whining.
agile—quick or nimble.
phlegmy—full of thick mucus.

Ulysses <u>unslung</u> from his belt a full <u>flask</u> of unwatered wine. He gave it to the giant, who put it to his lips and gulped. He coughed violently and stuck the sailor in a little <u>niche</u> high up in the cave wall, then leaned his great slab of a face toward Ulysses and said:

"What did you say this drink was?"

"Wine. A gift of the gods to man, to make women look better and food taste better. And now it is my gift to you."

"It's good, very good." He put the flask to his lips and swallowed again. "You are very polite. What's your name?"

"My name? Why I am—nobody."

"Nobody . . . Well, Nobody, I like you. You're a good fellow. And do you know what I'm going to do? I'm going to save you till last. Yes, I'll eat all your friends first, and give you extra time, that's what I'm going to do."

Ulysses looked up into the great eye and saw that it was redder than ever. It was all a swimming redness. He had given the monster, who had never drunk spirits before, <u>undiluted</u> wine. Surely it must make him sleepy. But was a gallon enough for that great <u>gullet</u>? Enough to put him to sleep—or would he want to eat again first?

"Eat 'em all up, Nobody—save you till later. Sleep a little first. Shall I? Won't try to run away, will you? No—you can't, can't open the door—too heavy, ha, ha. . . . You take a nap, too, Nobody. I'll wake you for breakfast. Breakfast . . . ."

VOCABULARY

unslung—took off.
flask—small container with a narrow neck used for holding water or wine.
niche—cranny, hollow, or crevice.
undiluted—not watered down; full strength.
gullet—throat.

The great body crashed full-length on the cave floor, making the very walls of the mountain shake. Polyphemus lay on his back, snoring like a powersaw. The sailors were still on the floor, almost dead from fear.

"Up!" cried Ulysses. "Stand up like men! Do what must be done! Or you will be devoured like chickens."

He got them to their feet and drew them about him as he explained his plan.

"Listen now, and listen well, for we have no time. I made him drunk, but we cannot tell how long it will last."

Ulysses thrust his sword into the fire; they saw it glow white-hot.

"There are ten of us," he said. "Two of us have been eaten, and one of our friends is still unconscious up there on his shelf of rock. You four get on one side of his head, and the rest on the other side. When I give the word, lay hold of the ear on your side, each of you. And hang on, no matter how he <u>thrashes</u>, for I am going to put out his eye. And if I am to be sure of my stroke, you must hold his head still. One stroke is all I will be allowed."

Then Ulysses rolled a boulder next to the giant's head and climbed on it, so that he was looking down into the eye. It was lidless and misted with sleep—big as a furnace door and glowing softly like a banked fire. Ulysses looked at his men. They had done what he said, broken into two parties, one group at each ear. He lifted his white-hot sword.

VOCABULARY
thrashes—moves about wildly and violently.

"Now!" he cried.

Driving down with both hands and all the strength of his back and shoulders and all his rage and all his fear, Ulysses stabbed the glowing spike into the giant's eye.

His sword jerked out of his hand as the head flailed upward; men pelted to the ground as they lost their hold. A huge screeching, curdling bellow split the air.

stop + predict

What do you predict will happen to Ulysses and his men now?

....

....

....

stop + predict

"This way!" shouted Ulysses.

He motioned to his men, and they crawled on their bellies toward the far end of the cave where the herd of goats was tethered. They slipped into the herd and lay among the goats as the giant stomped about the cave, slapping the walls with great blows of his hands, picking up boulders and cracking them together in agony, splitting them to cinders, clutching his eye, a scorched hole now, from which the brown blood jelled. He moaned and gibbered and bellowed in frightful pain; his groping hand found the sailor in the wall, and he tore him to pieces between his fingers. Ulysses could not even hear the man scream because the giant was bellowing so.

Now Ulysses saw that the Cyclops' wild stampeding was giving place to a plan. For now he was stamping on the floor in a regular pattern, trying to find and crush them beneath his feet. He stopped moaning and

VOCABULARY
flailed—moved wildly and vigorously about.
bellow—roar of a large animal.
tethered—held by a rope or chain.
cinders—small burned material, such as coal that cannot be burned further.

listened. The sudden silence dazed the men with fear. They held their breath and tried to muffle the sound of their beating hearts; all the giant heard was the breathing of the goats. Then Ulysses saw him go to the mouth of the cave and swing the great slab aside and stand there. He realized just in time that the goats would rush outside, which is what the giant wanted, for then he could search the whole cave.

Ulysses whispered: "Quickly, swing under the bellies of the rams. Hurry, hurry!"

Luckily, they were giant goats and thus able to carry the men who had swung themselves under their bellies and were clinging to the wiry wool. Ulysses himself chose the largest ram. They moved toward the mouth of the cave and crowded through. The Cyclops' hands came down and brushed across the goats' backs feeling for the men, but the animals were huddled too closely together for him to reach between and search under their bellies. So he let them pass through.

Now the Cyclops rushed to the corner where the goats had been tethered and stamped, searched, and roared through the whole cave again, bellowing with fury when he did not find them. The herd grazed on the slope of the hill beneath the cave. There was a full moon; it was almost bright as day.

"Stay where you are," Ulysses whispered.

He heard a crashing, peered out, and saw great shadowy figures <u>converging</u> on the cave. He knew that the other Cyclopes of the island must have heard the noise and had come to see. He heard the giant bellow.

The others called to him: "Who has done it? Who has blinded you?"

"Nobody. Nobody did it. Nobody blinded me."

"Ah, you have done it yourself. What a tragic accident."

And they went back to their own caves.

"Now!" said Ulysses. "Follow me!"

He swung himself out from under the belly of the ram and raced down the hill. The others raced after him. They were halfway across the valley when they heard great footsteps rushing after them, and Polyphemus bellowing nearer and nearer.

"He's coming!" cried Ulysses. "Run for your lives!"

Fill in this story frame about what has happened so far in "The Cyclops' Cave." What happened first? What happened second? What happened third?

Story Frame

1	2	3

VOCABULARY

converging—coming together from different directions.

They ran as they had never run before, but the giant could cover fifty yards at a stride. It was only because he could not see and kept bumping into trees and rocks that they were able to reach the <u>skiff</u> and push out on the silver water before Polyphemus burst out of the grove of trees and rushed onto the beach. They bent to the oars, and the boat scudded toward the fleet.

Polyphemus heard the dip of the oars and the groaning of the oarlocks and, aiming at the sound, hurled huge boulders after them. They fell all around the ship but did not hit. The skiff reached Ulysses' ship, and the sailors climbed aboard.

"Haul anchor, and away!" cried Ulysses. And then called to the Cyclops: "Poor fool! Poor blinded, drunken, <u>gluttonous</u> fool—if anyone else asks you, it is not Nobody, but Ulysses who has done this to you."

But he was to regret this final <u>taunt</u>. The gods honor courage but punish pride.

Polyphemus, wild with rage, waded out chest-deep and hurled a last boulder, which hit mid-deck, almost sunk the ship, and killed most of the crew—among them seven of the nine men who had just escaped.

And Polyphemus prayed to Poseidon: "God of the Sea, I beg you, punish Ulysses for this. Visit him with storm and shipwreck and <u>sorceries</u>. Let him wander many years before he reaches home, and when he gets there let him find himself forgotten, unwanted, a stranger."

Poseidon heard this prayer and made it all happen just that way.

VOCABULARY

skiff—flat-bottomed open boat.
gluttonous—having a large, excessive appetite.
taunt—scornful or sarcastic remark.
sorceries—supernatural powers; witchcraft.

GATHER YOUR THOUGHTS

CLARIFY PLOT Use this storyboard to show the sequence of events in "The Cyclops' Cave." Draw a picture and write a caption in each frame.

1

2

3

4

5

6

IV. WRITE

Get ready to write a **short story** about Ulysses.

1. First reread the final two paragraphs of "The Cyclops' Cave."
2. Next write the story of the "storm," "shipwreck," or "sorcery" that Poseidon will create to punish Ulysses.
3. Begin your story with the sentence below. ┈┈┈┈┈┈┈┈
4. Use the Writers' Checklist to help you revise.

After careful thought, Poseidon came up with a way to punish Ulysses for his pride.

WRITERS' CHECKLIST

VERBS

Present tense verbs show action that is happening now: *sail, yell,* and *cry.* Past tense verbs show action that happened before: *sailed, yelled,* and *cried.* The future tense shows action that will happen in the future: *will sail, will yell, will cry.*

☐ Did you stick to past tense verbs in your story?

☐ Did your verbs help the reader keep track of when events happen?

V. WRAP-UP

After you read, reflect back on what you liked or disliked about a selection. Write 2 or 3 sentences that explain whether or not you liked "The Cyclops' Cave."

READERS' CHECKLIST

ENQOYMENT

☐ Did you like the reading?

☐ Was the reading experience pleasurable?

☐ Would you want to reread the piece or recommend it to someone?

10: Hercules

Who are your heroes? Throughout the ages people have written about those they admire—men and women of great courage and strong character. Hercules was one such hero of ancient Greek and Roman myths.

BEFORE YOU READ

Read each sentence below aloud with one or more partners. The sentences come from the myth "Hercules."

1. Decide which one comes first in the story, which one second, and so on. Number them.

2. Then explain what the sentences make you think the story will be about.

_____ "HE WAS NEVER TRANQUIL AND AT EASE."

_____ "'SO I WILL DIE,' SAID HERCULES."

_____ "THEN HIS SANITY RETURNED. HE FOUND HIMSELF IN HIS BLOODSTAINED HALL, THE DEAD BODIES OF HIS SONS AND HIS WIFE BESIDE HIM."

_____ "THIS WAS THE FIRST TIME HE DEALT A FATAL BLOW WITHOUT INTENDING IT."

_____ "THE ELEVENTH LABOR WAS THE MOST DIFFICULT OF ALL SO FAR."

What do you think "Hercules" will be about?

....

....

....

....

....

....

....

....

....

II. READ

Read this excerpt from "Hercules" at your own pace.

1. Underline or **highlight** information about Hercules.

2. Put a star (⭐) in the margin whenever you learn something about his thoughts or feelings.

Response Notes

"Hercules" by Edith Hamilton

Great care was taken with his education, but teaching him what he did not wish to learn was a dangerous business. He seems not to have liked music, which was a most important part of a Greek boy's training, or else he disliked his music master. He flew into a rage with him and brained him with his <u>lute</u>. This was the first time he dealt a <u>fatal</u> blow without intending it. He did not mean to kill the poor musician; he just struck out on the <u>impulse</u> of the moment without thinking, hardly aware of his strength. He was sorry, very sorry, but that did not keep him from doing the same thing again and again. The other subjects he was taught, fencing, wrestling, and driving, he took to more kindly, and his teachers in these branches all survived. By the time he was eighteen he was full-grown and he killed, alone by himself, a great lion which lived in the woods of Cithaeron, the Thespian lion. Ever after he wore its skin as a cloak with the head forming a kind of hood over his own head.

EXAMPLE:
dislikes learning music and has a temper ⭐

stop + think

What three words would you use to describe Hercules?

1. _____   2. _____   3. _____

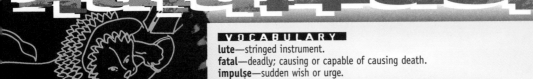

stop + think

VOCABULARY
lute—stringed instrument.
fatal—deadly; causing or capable of causing death.
impulse—sudden wish or urge.

"Hercules" continued

His next exploit was to fight and conquer the Minyans, who had been exacting a burdensome tribute from the Thebans. The grateful citizens gave him as a reward the hand of the Princess Megara. He was devoted to her and to their children and yet this marriage brought upon him the greatest sorrow of his life as well as trials and dangers such as no one ever went through, before or after. When Megara had borne him three sons he went mad. Hera who never forgot a wrong sent the madness upon him. He killed his children and Megara, too, as she tried to protect the youngest. Then his sanity returned. He found himself in his bloodstained hall, the dead bodies of his sons and his wife beside him. He had no idea what had happened, how they had been killed. Only a moment since, as it seemed to him, they had all been talking together. As he stood there in utter bewilderment the terrified people who were watching him from a distance saw that the mad fit was over, and Amphitryon dared to approach him. There was no keeping the truth from Hercules. He had to know how this horror had come to pass and Amphitryon told him. Hercules heard him out; then he said, "And I myself am the murderer of my dearest."

"Yes,"' Amphitryon answered trembling. "But you were out of your mind."

Hercules paid no attention to the implied excuse.

"Shall I spare my own life then?" he said. "I will avenge upon myself these deaths."

But before he could rush out and kill himself, even as he started to do so, his desperate purpose was changed and his life was spared. This miracle—it was nothing less—of recalling Hercules, from frenzied

VOCABULARY
exploit—act or deed.
Hera—wife of the god Zeus and queen of Heaven.
sanity—ability to think clearly; good judgment; soundness of mind.
bewilderment—confusion.
frenzied—wildly excited or crazy with excitement.

feeling and violent action to sober reason and sorrowful acceptance, was not wrought by a god descending from the sky. It was a miracle caused by human friendship. His friend Theseus stood before him and stretched out his hands to clasp those bloodstained hands. Thus according to the common Greek idea he would himself become <u>defiled</u> and have a part in Hercules' guilt.

"Do not start back," he told Hercules. "Do not keep me from sharing all with you. Evil I share with you is not evil to me. And hear me. Men great of soul can bear the blows of heaven and not flinch."

Hercules said, "Do you know what I have done?"

"I know this," Theseus answered. "Your sorrows reach from earth to heaven."

"So I will die," said Hercules.

"No hero spoke those words," Theseus said.

"What can I do but die?" Hercules cried. "Live? A branded man for all to say, 'Look. There is he who killed his wife and sons! Everywhere my jailers, the sharp <u>scorpions of the tongue</u>!"

"Even so, suffer and be strong," Theseus answered. "You shall come to Athens with me, share my home and all things with me. And you will give to me and to the city a great return, the glory of having helped you."

stop+think

Why did Hercules kill his family?

....

....

A long silence followed. At last Hercules spoke, slow, heavy words. "So let it be," he said, "I will be strong and wait for death."

VOCABULARY
defiled—made filthy, dirty, or polluted.
scorpions of the tongue—liars who slay with their false words.

"Hercules" continued

The two went to Athens, but Hercules did not stay there long. Theseus, the thinker, rejected the idea that a man could be guilty of murder when he had not known what he was doing and that those who helped such a one could be reckoned defiled. The Athenians agreed and welcomed the poor hero. But he himself could not understand such ideas. He could not think the thing out at all; he could only feel. He had killed his family. Therefore he was defiled and a defiler of others. He deserved that all should turn from him with <u>loathing</u>. At Delphi where he went to consult the <u>oracle</u>, the priestess looked at the matter just as he did. He needed to be purified, she told him, and only a terrible <u>penance</u> could do that. She <u>bade</u> him go to his cousin Eurystheus, King of Mycenae (of Tiryns in some stories) and submit to whatever he demanded of him. He went willingly, ready to do anything that could make him clean again. It is plain from the rest of the story that the priestess knew what Eurystheus was like and that he would beyond question purge Hercules thoroughly.

Eurystheus was by no means stupid, but of a very <u>ingenious</u> turn of mind, and when the strongest man on earth came to him humbly prepared to be his slave, he devised a series of penances which from the point of view of difficulty and danger could not have been improved upon. It must be said, however, that he was helped and urged on by Hera. To the end of Hercules' life she never forgave him for being Zeus's son. The tasks Eurystheus gave him to do are called "the Labors of Hercules." There were twelve of them and each one was all but impossible.

The first was to kill the lion of Nemea, a beast no weapons could wound. That difficulty Hercules solved

VOCABULARY

loathing—hatred.
oracle—priest who is consulted for his or her opinions and foretells the future.
penance—sacrifice made to pay for one's sins.
bade—asked or commanded.
ingenious—clever; marked by imaginative skill or imagination.

by choking the life out of him. Then he heaved the huge carcass up on his back and carried it into Mycenae. After that, Eurystheus, a cautious man, would not let him inside the city. He gave him his orders from afar.

stop+think

Why does Hercules agree to perform the twelve labors?

....

....

stop+think

The second labor was to go to Lerna and kill a creature with nine heads called the Hydra which lived in a swamp there. This was exceedingly hard to do, because one of the heads was <u>immortal</u> and the others almost as bad, inasmuch as when Hercules chopped off one, two grew up instead. However, he was helped by his nephew Iolaus who brought him a burning brand with which he seared the neck as he cut each head off so that it could not <u>sprout</u> again. When all had been chopped off he disposed of the one that was immortal by burying it securely under a great rock.

The third labor was to bring back alive a stag with horns of gold, sacred to Artemis, which lived in the forests of Cerynitia. He could have killed it easily, but to take it alive was another matter and he hunted it a whole year before he succeeded.

The fourth labor was to capture a great boar which had its lair on Mount Erymanthus. He chased the beast from one place to another until it was exhausted; then he drove it into deep snow and trapped it.

The fifth labor was to clean the Augean <u>stables</u> in a single day. Augeas had thousands of cattle and their

VOCABULARY
immortal—unable to die; able to live forever.
sprout—spring up or grow out.
stables—building used to shelter animals, especially horses.

"Hercules" continued

stalls had not been cleared out for years. Hercules diverted the courses of two rivers and made them flow through the stables in a great flood that washed out the filth in no time at all.

The sixth labor was to drive away the Stymphalian birds, which were a plague to the people of Stymphalus because of their enormous numbers. He was helped by Athena to drive them out of their coverts, and as they flew up he shot them.

The seventh labor was to go to Crete and fetch from there the beautiful savage bull that Poseidon had given Minos. Hercules mastered him, put him in a boat and brought him to Eurystheus.

The eighth labor was to get the man-eating mares of King Diomedes of Thrace. Hercules slew Diomedes first and then drove off the mares unopposed.

stop+think

What are the labors up to this point in the story? List them in order.

1. _____   5. _____

2. _____   6. _____

3. _____   7. _____

4. _____   8. _____

stop+think

The ninth labor was to bring back the girdle of Hippolyta, the Queen of the Amazons. When Hercules arrived she met him kindly and told him she would give him the girdle, but Hera stirred up trouble. She made the Amazons think that Hercules was going to carry off their queen, and they charged down on his ship. Hercules, without a thought of how kind Hippolyta had been, without any thought at all, instantly killed her, taking it for granted that she was

VOCABULARY
plague—widespread problem.
mares—female horses.

responsible for the attack. He was able to fight off the others and get away with the girdle.

The tenth labor was to bring back the cattle of Geryon, who was a monster with three bodies living on Erythia, a western island. On his way there Hercules reached the land at the end of the Mediterranean and he set up as a memorial of his journey two great rocks, called the pillars of Hercules (now Gibraltar and Ceuta). Then he got the oxen and took them to Mycenae.

Character Analysis

What do you know about the character of Hercules? Make some notes on this chart. Then finish reading the story.

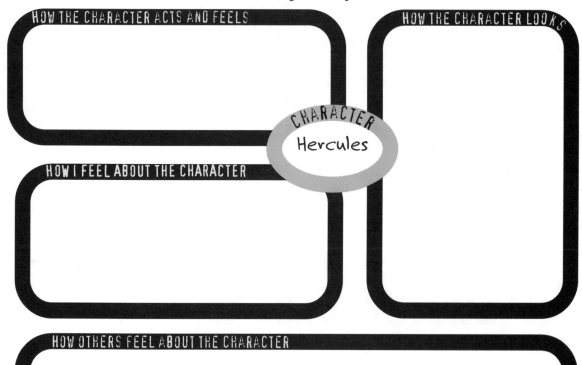

HOW THE CHARACTER ACTS AND FEELS

HOW THE CHARACTER LOOKS

HOW I FEEL ABOUT THE CHARACTER

CHARACTER
Hercules

HOW OTHERS FEEL ABOUT THE CHARACTER

The eleventh labor was the most difficult of all so far. It was to bring back the Golden Apples of the Hesperides, and he did not know where they were to be

"Hercules" continued

found. Atlas, who bore the vault of heaven upon his shoulders, was the father of the Hesperides, so Hercules went to him and asked him to get the apples for him. He offered to take upon himself the burden of the sky while Atlas was away. Atlas, seeing a chance of being relieved forever from his heavy task, gladly agreed. He came back with the apples, but he did not give them to Hercules. He told Hercules he could keep on holding up the sky, for Atlas himself would take the apples to Eurystheus. On this occasion Hercules had only his wits to trust to; he had to give all his strength to supporting that mighty load. He was successful, but because of Atlas' stupidity rather than his own cleverness. He agreed to Atlas' plan, but asked him to take the sky back for just a moment so that Hercules could put a pad on his shoulders to ease the pressure. Atlas did so, and Hercules picked up the apples and went off.

The twelfth labor was the worst of all. It took him down to the lower world, and it was then that he freed Theseus from the Chair of Forgetfulness. His task was to bring Cerberus, the three-headed dog, up from Hades. Pluto gave him permission provided Hercules used no weapons to overcome him. He could use his hands only. Even so, he forced the terrible monster to submit to him. He lifted him and carried him all the way up to the earth and on to Mycenae. Eurystheus very sensibly did not want to keep him and made Hercules carry him back. This was his last labor.

When all were completed and full expiation made for the death of his wife and children, he would seem to have earned ease and tranquillity for the rest of his life. But it was not so. He was never tranquil and at ease.

VOCABULARY
vault—arched structure that gives support, usually to a roof or ceiling.
submit—yield or surrender to the will of another.
expiation—act of paying for or making amends for one's sin.
tranquillity—peace; freedom from tension, restlessness, or anxiety.

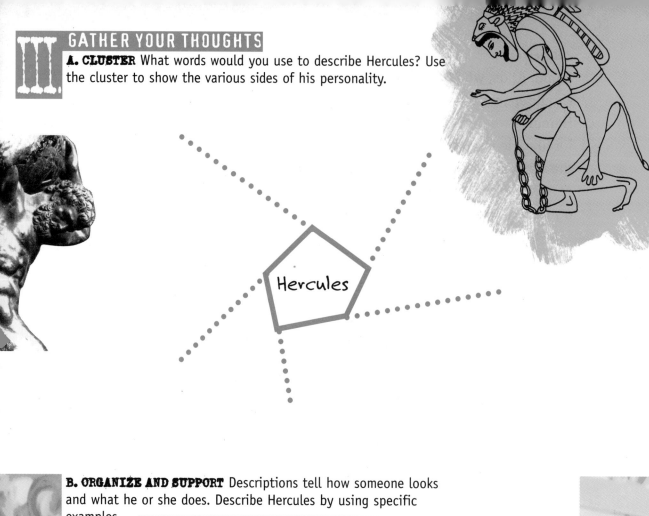

A. CLUSTER What words would you use to describe Hercules? Use the cluster to show the various sides of his personality.

Hercules

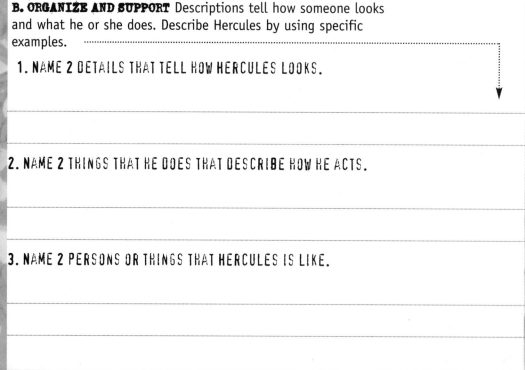

B. ORGANIZE AND SUPPORT Descriptions tell how someone looks and what he or she does. Describe Hercules by using specific examples.

1. NAME 2 DETAILS THAT TELL HOW HERCULES LOOKS.

2. NAME 2 THINGS THAT HE DOES THAT DESCRIBE HOW HE ACTS.

3. NAME 2 PERSONS OR THINGS THAT HERCULES IS LIKE.

IV. WRITE

Imagine a friend has asked you, "Who was Hercules?" Write a **character description paragraph.** Describe this famous character.

1. Begin with a topic sentence that makes a main point about Hercules.

2. Use the Writers' Checklist to help you revise.

WRITERS' CHECKLIST

SUBJECT-VERB AGREEMENT

The subject and verb of a sentence must work together, or agree. A sentence with a singular subject (Zeus) must have a singular verb (rules). A sentence with a plural subject (Zeus and Hera) must have a plural verb (rule).

EXAMPLES: Hercules *kills* the lion. Hercules and his friends *were* worried.

❑ Did you use plural verbs for all plural subjects?

❑ Did you use singular verbs for all singular subjects?

V. WRAP-UP

What made the tale of Hercules easy or difficult for you to read?

(blank lines for answer)

READERS' CHECKLIST

EASE

☐ Was the passage easy to read?

☐ Were you able to read it smoothly and without difficulty?

Dorothy West

Dorothy West

STORIES, SKETCHES AND REMINISCENCES

The Richer, the Poorer

Dorothy West
AUTHOR OF THE WEDDING

Dorothy West (1910–1998) has written fiction, newspaper columns, essays, and articles for literary magazines. *The Richer, the Poorer* (1995) is a collection of stories, sketches, and memoirs about African-American middle-class life.

11: **The Richer, the Poorer**

What is "rich," and what is "poor"? Sometimes when you read, you can better understand a story if you first explore the meaning of a key word or idea in the reading.

I. BEFORE YOU READ

In "The Richer, the Poorer," Dorothy West tells about two sisters who live very different lives.

1. Think about the title and what the words *richer* and *poorer* suggest.

2. Complete the chart below.

COMPARE AND CONTRAST CHART

RICHER	VS.	POORER

word to describe

phrase to describe

example of person

example of thing

II. READ

Read through the first part of the story at your own pace.

1. As you read, make **predictions** in the Response Notes about what you think will happen next.

2. Write **questions** about any part you don't understand or would like to ask the author about.

"The Richer, the Poorer" by Dorothy West

RESPONSE NOTES

Over the years Lottie had urged Bess to prepare for her old age. Over the years Bess had lived each day as if there were no other. Now they were both past sixty, the time for summing up. Lottie had a bank account that had never grown lean. Bess had the clothes on her back, and the rest of her worldly <u>possessions</u> in a battered suitcase.

Lottie had hated being a child, hearing her parents' <u>skimping</u> and scraping. Bess had never seemed to notice. All she ever wanted was to go outside and play. She learned to skate on borrowed skates. She rode a borrowed bicycle. Lottie couldn't wait to grow up and buy herself the best of everything.

> **EXAMPLE:**
> How could these two sisters be so different?

As soon as anyone would hire her, Lottie put herself to work. She minded babies, she ran errands for the old.

She never touched a penny of her money, though her child's mouth watered for ice cream and candy. But she could not bear to share with Bess, who never had anything to share with her. When the dimes began to add up to dollars, she lost her taste for sweets.

By the time she was twelve, she was <u>clerking</u> after school in a small <u>variety store</u>. Saturdays she worked as long as she was wanted. She decided to keep her money for clothes. When she entered high school, she would wear a <u>wardrobe</u> that neither she nor anyone else would be able to match.

▪ VOCABULARY ▪

possessions—material things that a person owns.
skimping—being stingy with.
clerking—working at a sales counter in a store.
variety store—store that sells toys, clothes, and everyday items.
wardrobe—all of the clothing belonging to a person.

But her freshman year found her unable to indulge so frivolous a whim, particularly when her admiring instructors advised her to think seriously of college. No one in her family had ever gone to college, and certainly Bess would never get there. She would show them all what she could do, if she put her mind to it.

She began to bank her money, and her bankbook became her most private and precious possession.

In her third year of high school she found a job in a small but expanding restaurant, where she cashiered from the busy hour until closing. In her last year of high school the business increased so rapidly that Lottie was faced with the choice of staying in school or working full time.

She made her choice easily. A job in hand was worth two in the future.

stop and think

What have you learned about Lottie up to this point?

_____

_____

What have you learned about her sister Bess?

_____

_____

Bess had a beau in the school band, who had no other ambition except to play a horn. Lottie expected to be settled with a home and family while Bess was still waiting for Harry to earn enough to buy a marriage license.

That Bess married Harry straight out of high school was not surprising. That Lottie never married at all was not really surprising either. Two or three times she was halfway persuaded, but to give up a job that paid well for a homemaking job that paid nothing was a risk she was incapable of taking.

VOCABULARY
cashiered—worked in a business as the person in charge of paying and receiving money.
ambition—dream, object, or goal that is desired.

Bess's married life was nothing for Lottie to envy. She and Harry lived like gypsies, Harry playing in second-rate bands all over the country, even getting himself and Bess stranded in Europe. They were often in rags and never in riches.

Bess grieved because she had no child, not having sense enough to know she was better off without one. Lottie was certainly better off without nieces and nephews to feel sorry for. Very likely Bess would have dumped them on her doorstep.

That Lottie had a doorstep they might have been left on was only because her boss, having bought a second house, offered Lottie his first house at a price so low and terms so reasonable that it would have been like losing money to refuse.

She shut off the rooms she didn't use, letting them go to rack and ruin. Since she ate her meals out, she had no food at home, and did not encourage callers, who always expected a cup of tea.

Her way of life was mean and miserly, but she did not know it. She thought she lived frugally in her middle years so that she could live in comfort and ease when she most needed peace of mind.

The years, after forty, began to race. Suddenly Lottie was sixty, and retired from her job by her boss's son, who had no sentimental feeling about keeping her on until she was ready to quit.

She made several attempts to find other employment, but her dowdy appearance made her look old and inefficient. For the first time in her life Lottie would gladly have worked for nothing, to have some place to go, something to do with her day.

Harry died abroad, in a third-rate hotel, with Bess weeping as hard as if he had left her a fortune. He had left her nothing but his horn. There wasn't even money for her passage home.

VOCABULARY

rack and ruin—a bad state in which things are completely worn out.
miserly—like a miser or person who lives meagerly
    in order to save money.

Lottie, trapped by the blood tie, knew she would not only have to send for her sister, but take her in when she returned. It didn't seem fair that Bess should reap the harvest of Lottie's lifetime of self-denial.

GATHER YOUR THOUGHTS

A. ORGANIZE DETAILS Dorothy West's story sets up a comparison in the title. Then she introduces two characters: Lottie and Bess.

1. Take a moment to organize some of the details the story has given you to this point about each woman.

2. List 3 details you have learned about each character.

LOTTIE

BESS

B. ORGANIZE A PARAGRAPH Make a plan for writing a paragraph that compares and contrasts the two sisters.

1. Study the two organizational plans below.

2. Choose one of the ways to organize your details and then fill out your plan.

1. ↓↓↓ORGANIZE BY ONE PERSON AND THEN THE OTHER↓↓↓

LOTTIE	**BESS**
Detail 1	Detail 1
Detail 2	Detail 2
Detail 3	Detail 3

2. ↓↓↓ORGANIZE BY TRAIT OR CHARACTERISTIC ↓↓

TRAIT 1:	TRAIT 2:	TRAIT 3:
Bess	Bess	Bess
Lottie	Lottie	Lottie

IV. WRITE

Now use your notes to create a **compare and contrast paragraph.**

1. Start your paragraph with a topic sentence about Bess and Lottie.
2. Use the Writers' Checklist to help you revise your paragraph.

Topic sentence: tells the main topic of the paragraph, prepares the reader

Details: support the topic sentence, give the most important ideas

Continue your writing on the next page.

WRITERS' CHECKLIST
COMMAS

❏ **Did you use a comma before the conjunctions *and, but, or, nor, yet,* and *for* when they combine two sentences?**
EXAMPLE: *Bess enjoyed her traveling, but she finally came home.*

❏ **Did you use a comma to separate three or more words, phrases, or clauses in a series?** EXAMPLE: *Lottie worked hard, saved her money, and lived a careful life.*

Continue your writing from the previous page.

Last sentence: sums up the rest of the information, draws a conclusion, or tells the point

WRAP-UP
What part, if any, of the story showed you how you might become a better writer?

READERS'
CHECKLIST
STYLE
☐ Did you find the passage well written?
☐ Are the sentences well constructed and the words well chosen?
☐ Does the style show you how to be a better writer?

What makes you truly happy? How do you know when you're happy? Dorothy West looks at these questions in her story.

BEFORE YOU READ

Here are four statements about the sisters, Bess and Lottie. Read each one.

1. Fill in the circle that shows how strongly you agree or disagree with the statement.

ANTICIPATION GUIDE

Bess foolishly wandered around the world with her husband.

STRONGLY DISAGREE ○ ○ ○ ○ ○ STRONGLY AGREE

Like many free spirits, Bess has few things but has enjoyed life.

STRONGLY DISAGREE ○ ○ ○ ○ ○ STRONGLY AGREE

Lottie lives a careful, comfortable, and good life.

STRONGLY DISAGREE ○ ○ ○ ○ ○ STRONGLY AGREE

Things like good clothes and a nice home are important to Lottie.

STRONGLY DISAGREE ○ ○ ○ ○ ○ STRONGLY AGREE

Lottie is the happier of the two sisters because of all she has.

STRONGLY DISAGREE ○ ○ ○ ○ ○ STRONGLY AGREE

---

2. Share your responses with a partner. Talk about why you marked the circles you did.

3. Based on your discussion and your reading of the first part of the story, make a prediction. How do you think the story "The Richer, the Poorer" will end?

The story will probably end . . .

....

....

....

....

....

READ

Now read the rest of the story at your own pace.

1. As you read, jot down your **reactions** in the Response Notes.

2. Use a double-entry journal to gather your thoughts about West's story.

DOUBLE-ENTRY JOURNAL

EXAMPLE:

▶ **QUOTE**

"... Lottie felt she deserved it more than Bess."

▶ **MY THOUGHTS**

I guess Lottie feels sorry for herself. Why?

RESPONSE NOTES

EXAMPLE:

She's working harder than I would!

"The Richer, the Poorer" (continued) by Dorothy West

It took Lottie a week to get a bedroom ready, a week of hard work and hard cash. There was everything to do, everything to replace or paint. When she was through the room looked so fresh and new that Lottie felt she deserved it more than Bess.

She would let Bess have her room, but the mattress was so lumpy, the carpet so worn, the curtains so threadbare that Lottie's conscience pricked her. She supposed she would have to redo that room, too, and went about doing it with an eagerness that she mistook for haste.

When she was through upstairs, she was shocked to see how dismal downstairs looked by comparison. She tried to ignore it, but with nowhere to go to escape it, the contrast grew more intolerable.

She worked her way from kitchen to parlor, persuading herself she was only putting the rooms to rights to give herself something to do. At night she slept like a child after a long and happy day of playing house. She was having more fun than she had ever had in her life. She was living each hour for itself.

VOCABULARY

intolerable—unbearable; impossible to stand or endure.
parlor—room in a home set apart for the entertainment of visitors.

© GREAT SOURCE. COPYING IS PROHIBITED.

There was only a day now before Bess would arrive. Passing her gleaming mirrors, at first with vague awareness, then with painful clarity, Lottie saw herself as others saw her, and could not stand the sight.

She went on a spending spree from the specialty shops to beauty salon, emerging transformed into a woman who believed in miracles.

DOUBLE-ENTRY JOURNAL

▶ QUOTE

"She was living each hour for itself."

▶ MY THOUGHTS

She was in the kitchen basting a turkey when Bess rang the bell. Her heart raced, and she wondered if the heat from the oven was responsible.

She went to the door, and Bess stood before her. Stiffly she suffered Bess's embrace, her heart racing harder, her eyes suddenly smarting from the onrush of cold air.

"Oh, Lottie, it's good to see you," Bess said, but saying nothing about Lottie's splendid appearance. Upstairs Bess, putting down her shabby suitcase, said, "I'll sleep like a rock tonight," without a word of praise for her lovely room. At the lavish table, top-heavy with turkey, Bess said, "I'll take light and dark, both," with no marveling at the size of the bird, or that there was turkey for two elderly women, one of them too poor to buy her own bread.

With the glow of good food in her stomach, Bess began to spill stories. They were rich with places and people, most of them lowly, all of them magnificent. Her

VOCABULARY
gleaming—flashing or glowing; shining.
clarity—clearness.
basting—moistening with liquid, as when the juices are poured over a turkey or roast.

RESPONSE NOTES

face reflected her telling, the joys and sorrows of her remembering, and above all, the love she lived by that enhanced the poorest place, the humblest person.

Then it was that Lottie knew why Bess had made no mention of her finery, or the shining room, or the twelve-pound turkey. She had not even seen them. Tomorrow she would see the room as it really looked, and Lottie as she really looked, and the warmed-over turkey in its second-day glory. Tonight she saw only what she had come seeking, a place in her sister's home and heart.

She said, "That's enough about me. How have the years used you?"

"It was me who didn't use them," said Lottie wistfully. "I saved for them. I saved for them. I forgot the best of them would go without my ever spending a day or a dollar enjoying them. That's my life story in those few words, a life never lived.

DOUBLE-ENTRY JOURNAL

▶ QUOTE   ▶ MY THOUGHTS

"How have the years used you?"
"It was me who didn't use them ..."

"Now it's too near the end to try."

Bess said, "To know how much there is to know is the beginning of learning to live. Don't count the years that are left us. At our time of life it's the days that count. You've too much catching up to do to waste a minute of a waking hour feeling sorry for yourself."

Lottie grinned, a real wide-open grin, "Well to tell the truth, I felt sorry for you. Maybe if I had any sense I'd feel sorry for myself, after all. I know I'm too old to kick up my heels, but I'm going to let you show me how. If I land on my head, I guess it won't matter; I feel giddy already, and I like it."

VOCABULARY
finery—fine things, such as clothing, dishes, and silverware.
giddy—lightheaded; dizzy with excitement.

GATHER YOUR THOUGHTS

A. FIND THE THEME What point do you think West is trying to make in her story? The point an author tries to make is the theme. Write the main theme of "The Richer, the Poorer" on the line below.

B. FIND SUPPORTING DETAILS On the lines below, write details from the story that support what you wrote above. Supporting details are the details that prove West's theme or explain why it makes sense to you. The supporting details come from the story, not from your own ideas.

WHAT DOES BESS SAY OR DO THAT SUPPORTS THIS THEME?

WHAT DOES LOTTIE SAY OR DO THAT EXPLAINS THIS THEME?

HOW HAVE THE CHARACTERS CHANGED? WHAT CHANGES IN THEM HELP SUPPORT THIS THEME?

C. ORGANIZE THE PARAGRAPH Now organize your thoughts in the chart below. First write your theme. Then put 3 main details that support this theme.

THEME:		
SUPPORTING DETAIL	SUPPORTING DETAIL	SUPPORTING DETAIL

IV. WRITE

Write a **paragraph** explaining in your own words the theme of West's story "The Richer, the Poorer."

1. State the theme in a topic sentence at the beginning of the paragraph.
2. Then offer 3 or 4 reasons in support of that theme.
3. Use the Writers' Checklist to help you revise.

V. WRAP-UP

What did the story make you think about?

Protest and Revolt

Dr. Martin Luther King, Jr.

Mohandas K. Gandhi

Over the course of history, people have sought to improve their lives and countries through protest and revolution. Protest and revolt can take many forms, from picketing and strikes to speeches and fasts.

Do you think a story about farm animals will be silly or serious? By answering that question, you made a prediction. Making predictions before you read can help you feel more involved in the story.

BEFORE YOU READ

Get together with a partner or in a small group.
1. Ask someone to read aloud the title and the first paragraph.
2. Answer the questions on the Prediction Guide on the next page.
3. Share your answers with others. Make notes about others' predictions.

"Animals Unite!" from *Animal Farm* by George Orwell

At one end of the big barn, on a sort of raised platform, Major was already ensconced on his bed of straw, under a lantern which hung from a beam. He was twelve years old and had lately grown rather stout, but he was still a majestic-looking pig, with a wise and benevolent appearance in spite of the fact that his tushes had never been cut. Before long the other animals began to arrive and make themselves comfortable after their different fashions. First came the three dogs, Bluebell, Jessie, and Pincher, and then the pigs, who settled down in the straw immediately in front of the platform. The hens perched themselves on the window-sills, the pigeons fluttered up to the rafters, the sheep and cows lay down behind the pigs and began to chew the cud. The two cart-horses, Boxer and Clover, came in together, walking very slowly and setting down their vast hairy hoofs with great care lest there should be some small animal concealed in the

VOCABULARY

ensconced—settled comfortably.
lantern—light that can be carried from place to place.
stout—large in body; fat.
benevolent—characterized by doing good.
cud—something held in the mouth and chewed.
hoofs—feet of an animal, especially a horse.

straw. Clover was a stout motherly mare approaching middle life, who had never quite got her figure back after her fourth <u>foal</u>. Boxer was an enormous beast, nearly <u>eighteen hands high</u>, and as strong as any two ordinary horses put together. A white stripe down his nose gave him a somewhat stupid appearance, and in fact he was not of first-rate intelligence, but he was universally respected for his steadiness of character and tremendous powers of work.

VOCABULARY
foal—young offspring of a horse.
eighteen hands high—about 72 inches or 6 feet tall (a hand is 4 inches).

YOUR NAME: _____

TITLE: _____

AUTHOR: _____

Read these predictions. Circle whether you strongly agree, agree, disagree, or strongly disagree with each statement.

1. A story about a pig will not be serious.
A. STRONGLY AGREE   B. AGREE   C. DISAGREE   D. STRONGLY DISAGREE

2. The funny names for the characters probably are important to the story.
A. STRONGLY AGREE   B. AGREE   C. DISAGREE   D. STRONGLY DISAGREE

3. The author talks about the animals like they are human for a reason.
A. STRONGLY AGREE   B. AGREE   C. DISAGREE   D. STRONGLY DISAGREE

4. The character Major, who is a pig, will be unlikable.
A. STRONGLY AGREE   B. AGREE   C. DISAGREE   D. STRONGLY DISAGREE

 READ

Take turns reading aloud the remainder of "Animals Unite!"
1. Clarify each time you come to a problem (or conflict), by making a comment in the Response Notes.
2. Note any **questions** you have.

"Animals Unite!" continued

RESPONSE NOTES

After the horses came Muriel, the white goat, and Benjamin, the donkey. Benjamin was the oldest animal on the farm, and the worst tempered. He seldom talked,

EXAMPLE:
Why not?
Will this be an
important detail?

and when he did, it was usually to make some cynical remark—for instance, he would say that God had given him a tail to keep the flies off, but that he would sooner have had no tail and no flies. Alone among the animals on the farm he never laughed. If asked why, he would say that he saw nothing to laugh at. Nevertheless, without openly admitting it, he was devoted to Boxer; the two of them usually spent their Sundays together in the small paddock beyond the orchard, grazing side by side and never speaking.

The two horses had just lain down when a brood of ducklings, which had lost their mother, filed into the barn, cheeping feebly and wandering from side to side to find some place where they would not be trodden on. Clover made a sort of wall round them with her great foreleg, and the ducklings nestled down inside it and promptly fell asleep. At the last moment Mollie, the foolish, pretty white mare who drew Mr. Jones's trap, came mincing daintily in, chewing at a lump of sugar. She took a place near the front and began flirting her white mane, hoping to draw attention to the red ribbons it was plaited with. Last of all came the cat, who looked round, as usual, for the warmest place, and finally squeezed herself in between Boxer and Clover; there she purred contentedly throughout Major's speech without listening to a word of what he was saying.

All the animals were now present except Moses, the tame raven, who slept on a perch behind the back door.

When Major saw that they had all made themselves comfortable and were waiting attentively, he cleared his throat and began:

VOCABULARY
cynical—scornful of the motives, virtue, or integrity of others.
paddock—fenced area near a stable where horses graze (eat grass).
brood—young of certain animals, such as ducks.
cheeping—faint, shrill sound made by a young bird.
trodden—walked over; trampled.
foreleg—either of the front legs of a horse.
mincing daintily—walking delicately or beautifully.
mane—long hair on the top of the neck of a horse.
plaited—braided.
raven—large bird with black feathers and a croaking cry.

"Comrades, you have heard already about the strange dream that I had last night. But I will come to the dream later. I have something else to say first. I do not think, comrades, that I shall be with you for many months longer, and before I die, I feel it my duty to pass on to you such wisdom as I have acquired. I have had a long life, I have had much time for thought as I lay alone in my stall, and I think I may say that I understand the nature of life on this earth as well as any animal now living. It is about this that I wish to speak to you.

"Now, comrades, what is the nature of this life of ours? Let us face it: our lives are miserable, laborious, and short. We are born, we are given just so much food as will keep the breath in our bodies, and those of us who are capable of it are forced to work to the last atom of our strength; and the very instant that our usefulness has come to an end we are slaughtered with hideous cruelty. No animal in England knows the meaning of happiness or leisure after he is a year old. No animal in England is free. The life of an animal is misery and slavery: that is the plain truth.

What is the main point Major is making? Is he serious?

....

....

"But is this simply part of the order of nature? Is it because this land of ours is so poor that it cannot afford a decent life to those who dwell upon it? No, comrades, a thousand times no! The soil of England is fertile, its

VOCABULARY
slaughtered—killed.
hideous—horrible.
cruelty—quality or condition of causing pain and suffering.
fertile—capable of growing or producing crops; abundant.

RESPONSE NOTES

climate is good, it is capable of affording food in abundance to an enormously greater number of animals than now inhabit it. This single farm of ours would support a dozen horses, twenty cows, hundreds of sheep—and all of them living in a comfort and a dignity that are now almost beyond our imagining. Why then do we continue in this miserable condition? Because nearly the whole of the produce of our labour is stolen from us by human beings. There, comrades, is the answer to all our problems. It is summed up in a single word—Man. Man is the only real enemy we have. Remove Man from the scene, and the root cause of hunger and overwork is abolished for ever.

"Man is the only creature that consumes without producing. He does not give milk, he does not lay eggs, he is too weak to pull the plough, he cannot run fast enough to catch rabbits. Yet he is lord of all the animals. He sets them to work, he gives back to them the bare minimum that will prevent them from starving, and the rest he keeps for himself. Our labor tills the soil, our dung fertilizes it, and  yet there is not one of us that owns more than his bare skin. You cows that I see before me, how many thousands of gallons of milk have you given during this

VOCABULARY
abundance—in great amount.
inhabit—live in or on.
abolished—done away with.
consumes—eats or drinks; uses up.
minimum—least amount possible.
fertilizes—nourishes; increases the capacity to produce.

last year? And what has happened to that milk which should have been breeding up sturdy calves? Every drop of it has gone down the throats of our enemies. And you hens, how many eggs have you laid in this last year, and how many of those eggs ever hatched into chickens? The rest have all gone to market to bring in money for Jones and his men. And you, Clover, where are those four foals you bore, who should have been the support and pleasure of your old age? Each was sold at a year old—you will never see one of them again. In return for your four <u>confinements</u> and all your labor in the fields, what have you ever had except your bare <u>rations</u> and a stall?

STOP AND THINK

Is the story what you expected? Explain your answer.

....

....

"And even the miserable lives we lead are not allowed to reach their <u>natural span</u>. For myself I do not grumble, for I am one of the lucky ones. I am twelve years old and have had over four hundred children. Such is the natural life of a pig. But no animal escapes the cruel knife in the end. You young <u>porkers</u> who are sitting in front of me, every one of you will scream your lives out at the block within a year. To that horror we all must come—cows, pigs, hens, sheep, everyone. Even the horses and the dogs have no better fate. You, Boxer, the very day that those great muscles of yours lose their power, Jones will sell you to the <u>knacker</u>, who will cut your throat and <u>boil you down for the foxhounds</u>. As

■ VOCABULARY
confinements—offspring. Major is referring back to Clover's foals.
rations—fixed portions of food.
natural span—normal lifetime.
porkers—baby pigs.
knacker—British term to describe the person who buys old, worn-out animals and kills them to sell as meat or for their hides.
boil you down for the foxhounds—kill for dog food.

131

for the dogs, when they grow old and toothless, Jones ties a brick round their necks and drowns them in the nearest pond.

"Is it not crystal clear, then, comrades, that all the evils of this life of ours spring from the tyranny of human beings? Only get rid of Man, and the produce of our labor would be our own. Almost overnight we could become rich and free. What then must we do? Why, work night and day, body and soul, for the overthrow of the human race! That is my message to you, comrades: Rebellion! I do not know when that Rebellion will come, it might be in a week or in a hundred years, but I know, as surely as I see this straw beneath my feet, that sooner or later justice will be done. Fix your eyes on that, comrades, throughout the short remainder of your lives! And above all, pass on this message of mine to those who come after you, so that future generations shall carry on the struggle until it is victorious.

"And remember, comrades, your resolution must never falter. No argument must lead you astray. Never listen when they tell you that Man and the animals have a common interest, that the prosperity of the one is the prosperity of the others. It is all lies. Man serves the interests of no creature except himself. And among us animals let there be perfect unity, perfect comradeship in the struggle. All men are enemies. All animals are comrades."

How do you feel about what Major is saying?

....

....

VOCABULARY

tyranny—government in which a single ruler has absolute power.
Rebellion—open, armed resistance to a government.
resolution—determination; decision about future actions.
falter—weaken or hesitate.
astray—away from the correct path.

III GATHER YOUR THOUGHTS

A. ORGANIZE IDEAS Use a graphic organizer to put together what you know so far about the plot and characters of "Animals Unite!"

1. On the left side, list problems Major describes.

2. Use the right side for his solutions.

Major's Speech

PROBLEM	SOLUTION

B. USE DESCRIPTIVE WORDS Look back at the selection.

1. Circle some of the descriptive words used to describe Major.

2. Write them below.

<<<<<<<<<<WORD LIST>>>>>>>>>>

IV. WRITE

Write a brief **descriptive paragraph** about Major.

1. Describe how Major looks, acts, and feels.

2. Explain whether, in your opinion, Major is or is not a good leader.

3. Use the Writers' Checklist to help you revise your paragraph.

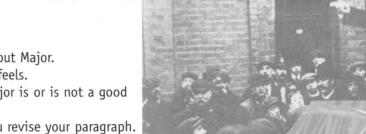

V. WRAP-UP

How would you explain in a few sentences the message in "Animals Unite!"?

READERS' CHECKLIST

UNDERSTANDING

☐ Did you understand the reading?

☐ Was the author's message or point clear?

☐ Can you restate what the reading is about?

How do the stories and articles you read apply to your own life? Do you ever ask yourself: "Have I had this experience?" or "What would I have done if this had been me?"

BEFORE YOU READ

"The Fast" is about a protest.

1. Quickwrite for 1 minute about the idea of protest. What do you feel strongly about? What would you protest for or against?

2. Get together in small groups and share your writing.

PROTEST

1-MINUTE QUICKWRITE

II. READ

With a partner, take turns reading "The Fast."
1. Write notes that **clarify** what you are reading.
2. In the Response Notes, note your **reactions** to what is happening.

"The Fast" from *An Autobiography*
by Mohandas K. Gandhi

For the first two weeks the mill-hands exhibited great courage and <u>self-restraint</u> and daily held monster meetings. On these occasions I used to remind them of their <u>pledge</u>, and they would shout back to me the <u>assurance</u> that they would rather die than break their word.

But at last they began to show signs of <u>flagging</u>. Just as physical weakness in men <u>manifests</u> itself in <u>irascibility</u>, their attitude towards the <u>blacklegs</u> became more and more menacing as the strike seemed to weaken, and I began to fear an outbreak of <u>rowdyism</u> on their part. The attendance at their daily meetings also began to <u>dwindle</u> by degrees, and <u>despondency</u> and despair were writ large on the faces of those who did attend. Finally the information was brought to me that the strikers had begun to <u>totter</u>. I felt deeply troubled and set to thinking furiously as to what my duty was in the circumstances. I had had experience of a gigantic strike in South Africa, but the situation that confronted me here was different. The mill-hands had taken the pledge at my suggestion. They had repeated it before me day after day, and the very idea that they might now go back upon it was to me <u>inconceivable</u>. Was it pride or was it my love for the

RESPONSE NOTES

EXAMPLE:
Strikers are becoming discouraged—
may become violent.

Mohandas K. Gandhi

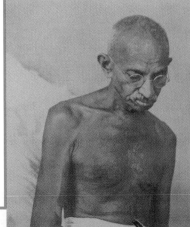

© GREAT SOURCE. COPYING IS PROHIBITED.

VOCABULARY
self-restraint—self-discipline.
pledge—promise.
assurance—promise.
flagging—declining in strength.
manifests—shows.
irascibility—outbursts of bad temper.
blacklegs—strike breakers.
rowdyism—disorderly conduct; fighting.
dwindle—become gradually less.
despondency—loss of hope.
totter—sway as if about to fall.
inconceivable—impossible to understand.

laborers and my passionate regard for truth that was at the back of this feeling—who can say?

One morning—it was at a mill-hands' meeting—while I was still groping and unable to see my way clearly, the light came to me. <u>Unbidden</u> and all by themselves the words came to my lips: "Unless the strikers rally," I declared to the meeting, "and continue the strike till a settlement is reached, or till they leave the mills altogether, I will not touch any food."

What will be the effect of Gandhi's statement? Explain your prediction.

_____

_____

The laborers were thunderstruck. Tears began to course down Anasuyabehn's cheeks. The laborers broke out, "Not you but we shall <u>fast</u>. It would be monstrous if you were to fast. Please forgive us for our lapse, we will now remain faithful to our pledge to the end."

"There is no need for you to fast," I replied. "It would be enough if you could remain true to your pledge. As you know we are without funds, and we do not want to continue our strike by living on public charity. You should therefore try to eke out a bare existence by some kind of labor, so that you may be able to remain unconcerned, no matter how long the strike may continue. As for my fast, it will be broken only after the strike is settled."

In the meantime Vallabhbhai was trying to find some employment for the strikers under the <u>Municipality</u>, but there was not much hope of success

VOCABULARY
Unbidden—not invited or asked.
fast—abstain or not take any food.
Municipality—city or town.

there. Maganlal Gandhi suggested that, as we needed sand for filling the foundation of our weaving school in the <u>Ashram</u>, a number of them might be employed for that purpose. The laborers welcomed the proposal. Anasuyabehn led the way with a basket on her head and soon an endless stream of laborers carrying baskets of sand on their heads could be seen issuing out of the <u>hollow</u> of the river-bed. It was a sight worth seeing. The laborers felt themselves infused with a new strength, and it became difficult to cope with the task of paying out wages to them.

My fast was not free from a <u>grave</u> defect. For as I have already mentioned in a previous chapter, I enjoyed very close and <u>cordial</u> relations with the mill-owners, and my fast could not but affect their decision. As a Satyagrahi I knew that I might not fast against them, but ought to leave them free to be influenced by the mill-hands' strike alone.

My fast was undertaken not on account of lapse of the mill-owners, but on account of that of the laborers in which, as their representative, I felt I had a share. With the mill-owners, I could only plead; to fast against them would amount to coercion. Yet in spite of my knowledge that my fast was bound to put pressure upon them, as in fact it did, I felt I could not help it. The duty to undertake it seemed to me to be clear.

VOCABULARY
Ashram—house of a religious community and its leader.
hollow—low area.
grave—serious; somber.
cordial—friendly.

I tried to set the mill-owners at ease. "There is not the slightest necessity for you to withdraw from your position," I said to them. But they received my words coldly and even flung keen, delicate bits of <u>sarcasm</u> at me, as indeed they had a perfect right to do.

The principal man at the back of the mill-owners' <u>unbending</u> attitude towards the strike was Sheth Ambalal. His <u>resolute</u> will and <u>transparent sincerity</u> were wonderful and captured my heart. It was a pleasure to be pitched against him. The strain produced by my fast upon the opposition, of which he was the head, cut me, therefore, to the quick. And then, Sarladevi, his wife, was attached to me with the affection of a blood-sister, and I could not bear to see her anguish on account of my action.

STOP AND THINK

What effect did Gandhi's fast have on others? Explain.

....

....

....

STOP AND THINK

Anasuyabehn and a number of other friends and laborers shared the fast with me on the first day. But after some difficulty I was able to dissuade them from continuing it further.

The net result of it was that an atmosphere of goodwill was created all round. The hearts of the mill-owners were touched, and they set about discovering some means for a settlement. Anasuyabehn's house became the <u>venue</u> of their

VOCABULARY

sarcasm—cutting, ironic remarks meant to wound.
unbending—not yielding or giving in.
resolute—firm or determined.
transparent sincerity—obvious honesty.
venue—place, scene, or setting.

"The Fast" continued

discussions. Sjt. Anandshankar Dhruva <u>intervened</u> and was in the end appointed <u>arbitrator</u>, and the strike was called off after I had fasted only for three days. The mill-owners <u>commemorated</u> the event by distributing sweets among the laborers, and thus a settlement was reached after 21 days' strike.

STORY FRAME

Complete this story frame for "The Fast."

1. THIS STORY TAKES PLACE IN

2. _____ IS THE MAIN CHARACTER IN THIS STORY

3. WHO IS

4. A PROBLEM OCCURS WHEN

5. AFTER THAT, HE

6. THE PROBLEM IS SOLVED WHEN

7. THE STORY ENDS WITH

VOCABULARY
intervened—entered into.
arbitrator—person chosen to help settle a dispute or argument.
commemorated—celebrated with a ceremony.

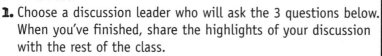

A. DISCUSS Stay in your reading group. Prepare for a discussion of "The Fast."

1. Choose a discussion leader who will ask the 3 questions below. When you've finished, share the highlights of your discussion with the rest of the class.
2. Take notes on the discussion in the boxes below.

Discussion question #1 **What made Gandhi a good leader?**

My notes:

Discussion question #2 **Why were people willing to follow him?**

My notes:

Discussion question #3 **Were you surprised by the effect of his fast? Why or why not?**

My notes:

B. BRAINSTORM Use your thoughts about "The Fast " to help you focus on a change you might want to lead people to make.
1. Write it in the center circle.
2. Brainstorm the details of the change and how you would convince people to support you. Write them on the lines below.

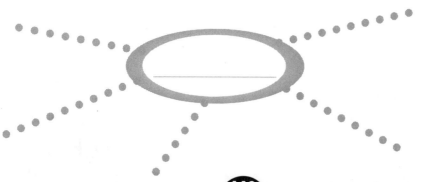

IV. WRITE

Imagine you are going to work for the change you wrote about on the previous page.

1. Write a **journal entry** that reveals what you want to do and how you would convince people to follow you.

2. Use the Writers' Checklist to help you revise.

Date:_____

WRITERS' CHECKLIST

APOSTROPHES

❏ Did you use an apostrophe in every contraction? *EXAMPLE: I'll work hard to make sure others don't forget their promises.*

❏ Did you put the apostrophe in the right place—where the letter(s) being left out would be? *EXAMPLE: She's (she is) not too happy I'm (I am) coming.*

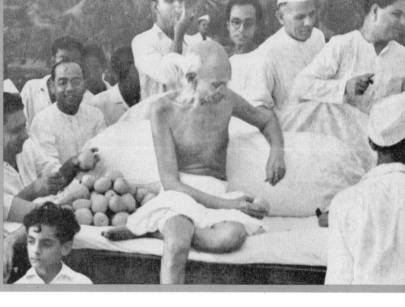

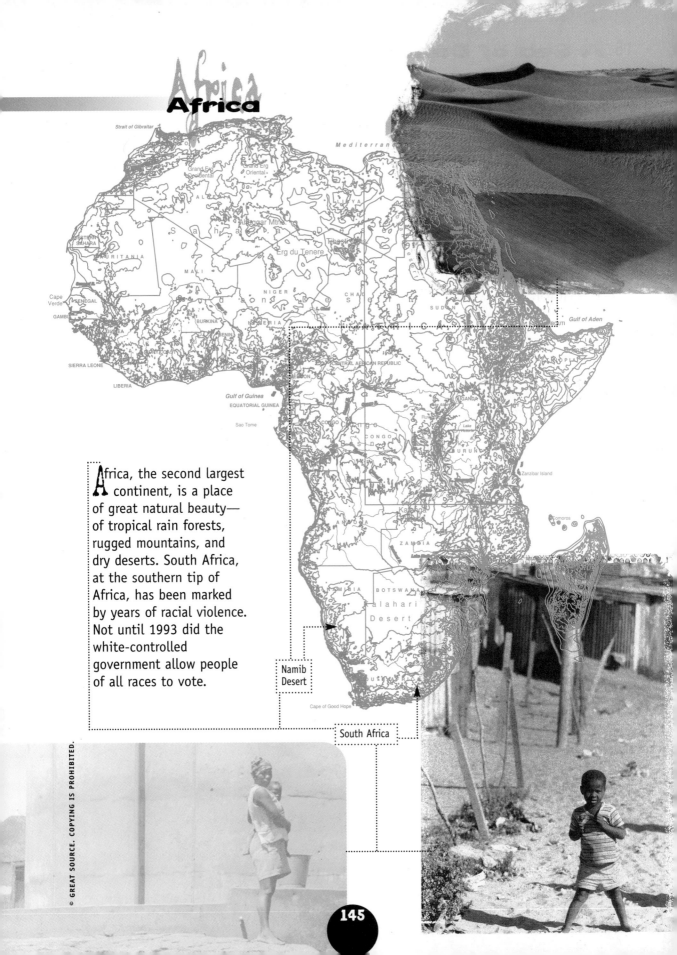

Africa, the second largest continent, is a place of great natural beauty— of tropical rain forests, rugged mountains, and dry deserts. South Africa, at the southern tip of Africa, has been marked by years of racial violence. Not until 1993 did the white-controlled government allow people of all races to vote.

Namib Desert

South Africa

Strait of Gibraltar
Mediterranean
Grand Erg Occidental
Grand Erg Oriental
ALGERIA
LIBYA
Ahaggar Mtns.
Sahara
Tibesti Mtns.
Erg du Tenere
WESTERN SAHARA
MAURITANIA
MALI
NIGER
CHAD
SUDAN
Cape Verde
SENEGAL
GAMBIA
GUINEA
BURKINA
NIGERIA
BENIN
SIERRA LEONE
LIBERIA
Gulf of Guinea
EQUATORIAL GUINEA
Sao Tome
CENTRAL AFRICAN REPUBLIC
Gulf of Aden
ETHIOPIA
UGANDA
CONGO
CONGO
BURUNDI
Lake
Zanzibar Island
Kananga
ANGOLA
ZAMBIA
Comoros
NAMIBIA
BOTSWANA
Kalahari Desert
Cape of Good Hope

15: A Sea of Dunes

Desert sands

What's your "recipe" for success? Nonfiction has certain ingredients, such as the title, chapter titles and headings, pictures, and captions. Looking at all these ingredients first helps prepare you to read.

BEFORE YOU READ

Read the title and the first paragraph of "A Sea of Dunes." It is part of a chapter in a book called *Sand and Fog*.

1. What part of the world does this article describe?

_____

_____

2. Now take a picture walk. Look at the photographs in the article and read the captions that go with them.

3. What do the photographs tell you about life in this place? Choose two photographs and record your ideas in the chart.

The photo of . . .	tells me . . .

The photo of . . .	tells me . . .

READ

Read "A Sea of Dunes."

1. Use the graphic organizer below to keep track of details about animal life in the Namib Desert.

2. Mark information that seems important and jot down any **questions** you have in the Response Notes.

Animals in the Namib Desert have different ways to adapt to their surroundings.

This is the main idea of the article. Look for different ways that animals adapt to living in the desert.

As you read, write the name of an animal in each column. Below the name, tell what the animal does to adapt to the desert.

Response Notes

"A Sea of Dunes" by Jim Brandenburg

How does life exist in the Namib Desert? The answer lies in the winds, and in the sea. And, ultimately, the ecosystem depends upon, of all things, fog.

The perpetually blowing winds are called "Soo-oop-wa" in one of the local languages. For countless centuries they have blown, modeling the vast sea of dunes into ever-changing linear waves, ridges and hollows, and cliffs of cascading sand. But the winds are more than just the sculptors of the Namib. For part of the year a hot, dry wind blows from the east bringing food—a scattering of organic particles from which desert plants draw nourishment.

EXAMPLE:

How big is it and how hot is it there?

VOCABULARY

Namib Desert—dry region of southwest Africa along the coast of Namibia.
ecosystem—ecological community together with its environment (that is, the world for an animal, insect, or other forms of life).
linear—of or relating to a line; straight.
cascading—falling in a series of stages, like a waterfall.
organic particles—microscopic bits of living material or matter.

At other times, warm Atlantic winds join forces with the cold current from <u>Antarctica</u>. The winds, charged with moisture, roll in to lay a <u>clammy shroud</u> of fog over the <u>coastal</u> desert.

It may not rain in this region for years, so the dense fog (which appears about one morning in every five) is the desert's only regular form of <u>precipitation</u>. Plants and animal life of the Namib have evolved in incredible ways to use these <u>meager</u> amounts of moisture in the form of mist or <u>dewdrops</u>.

The <u>oryx</u> I tracked drew nourishment *and* water from the desert grass and its precious <u>burden of dew</u>. Somehow, this is usually sufficient. An oryx is also remarkable for its ability to withstand the intense desert heat. Its body temperature rises so high that its blood could destroy the animal's brain cells. But, in a unique <u>adaptation</u>, blood destined for the brain is first cooled by <u>circulating</u> through a network of <u>capillaries</u> in the oryx's <u>nasal</u> passages.

stop + record

Oryx

You just found out how an <u>oryx</u> adapts to the desert.

☐ **Write** oryx **in the first column of the graphic organizer on page 147.**

☐ **Jot down a** few words **to tell how the oryx adapts to the desert.**

VOCABULARY

Antarctica—continent centered on the South Pole.
clammy shroud—wet, foggy covering.
coastal—lying along or next to an ocean or sea.
precipitation—water or moisture.
meager—very little.
dewdrops—water drops that gather in the cool night air and form on the surfaces of grass, stones, and other cool surfaces.
oryx—any of several African antelopes with long, slightly curved horns and a hump above the shoulders.
burden of dew—weight of the water collected in the form of a dewdrop.
adaptation—change in an animal to fit in with and live longer in its environment.
circulating—flowing.
capillaries—tiny blood vessels.
nasal—of or relating to the nose.

At least oryx can, and do, <u>migrate</u> to grassier regions. What about those creatures trapped in the desert?

They have evolved licking rather than drinking, as moisture beads up on plants, sand, even on the creatures themselves. The palmetto gecko (a type of lizard), for instance, licks moisture from its lidless eyes. And tiny black <u>beetles</u> stand almost on their heads, motionless on dune ridges, waiting for water droplets to accumulate on their bodies. Then, slowly, this moisture trickles down the insect's <u>grooved</u> back into its mouth.

stop + record

You just found out how <u>geckos</u> and <u>black beetles</u> adapt to the desert.

❏ **Write** each animal's name **in a column of the graphic organizer.**

❏ **Jot down a** few words **to tell how each animal adapts to the desert.**

❏ **Read ahead. Look for details about the <u>sidewinding adder</u> and the <u>sand grouse</u>.**

Camels provide transportation across the desert.

VOCABULARY

migrate—move from country to country or region to region.
beetles—insects with biting mouthparts and wings that form protective covering.
grooved—marked with a long, narrow channel or funnel.

"A Sea of Dunes" continued

Later in the day when the fog has lifted, these creatures, like most in the Namib, escape the heat by digging into the cool depths of the sand. The sidewinding adder finds not only coolness in the sand but also camouflage. This snake, which efficiently travels sideways across the hot, loose sand, lies in wait for prey, totally buried except for its eyes, which are set high on its head.

One of the more remarkable adaptations to desert dryness can be seen in the sand grouse. To fetch water for his chicks, the male parent flies up to fifty miles to a water hole, collects moisture in its thick breast feathers, and flies back. The waiting chicks then eagerly sip water from these still-wet feathers. This is only one of the daily miracles occurring in the region.

VOCABULARY

sidewinding adder—kind of desert snake.
camouflage—hiding by blending into the natural surroundings.
grouse—plump, chicken-like game bird.
miracles—events that appear impossible to explain by the laws of nature.

Sand sculpture of desert animals

GATHER YOUR THOUGHTS

How can you summarize the main points of the article? Follow this plan to get ready.

A. FIND THE MAIN IDEA A summary first states the main idea in a clear, brief way. Look back at the graphic organizer you began while reading the article. Rephrase the main idea in your own words and write it in the box below.

> **Main Idea**

B. ADD SUPPORTING DETAILS Next, find 2–4 details that support the main idea. Use the chart below to help organize them.

First, add a sentence telling what the conditions in the desert are like.

Next, give an example of how one animal adapts to life in the desert.

Then give one more example.

WHAT DESERT IS LIKE	EXAMPLE OF SURVIVAL	ANOTHER EXAMPLE

THE AUTHOR'S POINT WAS . . .

Finally, end with a sentence that concludes the paragraph.

IV. WRITE

Write a **summary** of "A Sea of Dunes."
1. Follow the plan below as you draft your paragraph.
2. Use the Writers' Checklist to help you revise.

```
┌─────────────────────────────────────────────┐
│              TOPIC SENTENCE                   │
├──────────────┬──────────────┬────────────────┤
│  SUPPORTING  │  SUPPORTING  │   SUPPORTING    │
│    DETAIL    │    DETAIL    │    DETAIL       │
├──────────────┴──────────────┴────────────────┤
│                CONCLUSION                      │
└─────────────────────────────────────────────┘
```

V. WRAP-UP

What parts of this article were difficult or easy for you to read? Explain.

16: The Widows of the Reserves

Reading is not something that you have to do all alone. When you read, you have a "conversation" with the writer. You can also read right along with other readers. When you ask someone else questions and share your ideas while you read, you can better understand what you are reading.

BEFORE YOU READ

Think about the title of this selection and what it may mean.

1. Then get in a group with 2–3 other students. Discuss the title. Next each group member should read one of the sentences below taken from the essay.

2. Talk about what each sentence means and write answers for the questions below.

think-pair-and-share

a. "The fortunate ones milk and shut in the stock, but for most there is no stock to shut in, and their children do not know the milk from the family cow."

b. "The rest of the evening is spent in silence."

c. "Widowhood—a life of void and loneliness; a period of tension, unbalance and strenuous adjustment."

d. "There will be bread, sugar, tea and a few extras for at least a few weeks. For others it is bad news."

Which sentence appears first in the story? Which one appears last?

What can you learn about the "widows" from these sentences?

How are the widows' lives like or unlike yours?

READ

Now read the rest of this excerpt from "The Widows of the Reserves" at your own pace. ⋯⋯⋯⋯⋯⋯

1. Try to **visualize** what is being described. Make sketches or drawings in the Response Notes as you read.

2. Mark or **highlight** passages that you find especially interesting or surprising.

Response Notes

EXAMPLE:

"The Widows of the Reserves" by Phyllis Ntantala

South Africa

Widowhood—a life of <u>void</u> and loneliness; a period of tension, unbalance and <u>strenuous</u> adjustment. And what can it be to those thousands of African women—those <u>adolescent</u> girls married before they reach womanhood, thrown into a life of responsibility before they have completely passed from childhood to adulthood; those young women in the <u>prime</u> of early womanhood left to face life alone, burdened with the task of building a home and rearing a family; those young women doomed to nurse alone their sick babies, weep alone over their dead babies, dress and bury alone their <u>corpses</u>? What can it mean to those young brides whose purpose has been snatched away, overnight, leaving them <u>bewildered</u> and lost, leaving them with a thirst and hunger that cannot be stilled?

And yet this is the daily lot of tens of thousands of African women whose husbands are torn away from them to go and work in the cities, mines and farms—husbands who because of the <u>migratory labor system</u> cannot take their wives with them and, because of the <u>starvation</u> wages they receive, are forced to remain in the work centers for long periods—strangers in a

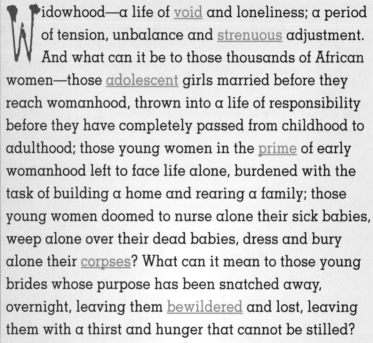

> **VOCABULARY**
> **void**—emptiness; empty space.
> **strenuous**—requiring great effort or energy.
> **adolescent**—young; not yet mature.
> **prime**—age of physical perfection; best or most perfect time of life.
> **corpses**—dead bodies.
> **bewildered**—confused.
> **migratory labor system**—way workers must constantly move about from place to place in order to work.
> **starvation**—condition of suffering and almost dying from lack of food.

"The Widows of the Reserves" continued

strange land—but equally strangers at home to their wives and children.

These women remain alone in the <u>Reserves</u> to build the homes, till the land, rear the <u>stock</u>, bring up the children. They watch alone the ravages of <u>drought</u>, when the <u>scraggy</u> cows cease to provide the milk, when the few stock drop one by one because there is no grass on the <u>veld</u>, and all the streams have been lapped dry by the scorching sun. They watch alone the crops in the fields wither in the <u>scorching</u> sun, their labor of months blighted in a few days. They witness alone the hailstorm sweep clean their <u>mealie lands</u>, alone they witness the wind lift bodily their huts as if they were pieces of paper, rendering them and their children homeless. Alone they bury their babies one by one and lastly their unknown lovers—their husbands, whose corpses alone are sent back to the Reserves. For the world of grinding machines has no use for men whose lungs are riddled with <u>t.b. and miner's phthisis</u>.

For miles around throughout the country one sees nobody but these women—young and yet stern-faced with lines of care on their faces. This one climbing the slope with a bucket of water on her head and, if lucky, a baby on her back; that one going up the hill with a heavy bundle of wood on her head; another following behind a span of six oxen drawing a sledge with <u>ploughing</u> <u>implements</u> and only a youngster of ten or twelve years as her help; and yet another driving home

VOCABULARY
Reserves—parts of the country set aside as public land.
stock—all of the animals kept or raised on a farm; livestock.
drought—long period of unusually low rainfall.
scraggy—bony and lean.
veld—open grazing area in southern Africa.
scorching—withering because of intense heat.
mealie lands—lands planted with corn.
t.b. and miner's phthisis—tuberculosis, a disease of the lungs, and phthisis, a disease that causes one to waste away. Both are deadly diseases.
ploughing—(also spelled *plowing*) breaking and turning over the earth with a metal blade to prepare ground for crops.
implements—tools or instruments.

a scraggy herd of cattle or a flock of sheep numbering twenty at the very most, with yet another small boy by her side.

In the ploughing season they are to be seen behind the span of oxen, holding the plough, leading the team of ploughing oxen. In the cold winter months, alone with young girls and boys they reap the fields, load the wagons and bring in the harvest. A poor harvest! What else could it be? "Bad farming methods of the native," is the official attitude of South Africa. But how could it be otherwise when the farming is left to women and children, when the whole task of homebuilding is on their shoulders?

stop + think

What makes farming difficult for the women?

Are methods of farming to blame for their problems? Explain why or why not.

stop + think

At home in the morning these lonely women see to it that their children get ready for school—those underfed and scantily dressed children whose breakfast is a piece of dry bread, mealie-pap without any milk, and for many just cold mush and beans. Their desire to see their children educated is so great that the women themselves go out with the stock in order to keep their children at school—to give them the education that will free them from poverty, the education that has given the other races so much knowledge and power.

VOCABULARY

scantily—barely enough; meagerly.
mealie-pap—soft, almost liquid mix of cornmeal and water, often eaten by infants.
mush—thick slice of cornmeal boiled in milk or water.

stop+think

How do they hope to free themselves of poverty?

stop+think

"The Widows of the Reserves" continued

Response Notes

At the close of day they light their fires to prepare the evening meal. The fortunate ones milk and shut in the stock, but for most there is no stock to shut in, and their children do not know the milk from the family cow. For some there is a letter of good news from the father and husband far away in the work center—the long-awaited letter with money has come—part of the debt at the trader's will be paid off. There will be bread, sugar, tea and a few extras to eat for at least a few weeks. For others it is bad news. The loved one far away is ill, has met with an accident, has been thrown into jail because he failed to produce his papers when demanded by some government official. Not that he did not have them, but just that by mistake he forgot them in the pocket of his other jacket. A black man in South Africa cannot forget! It is a sad day for this one. Her children look up anxiously in her face. They fear to ask her any questions, and she does not know how much to tell them. "Tata sends his greetings," she manages to say at last, "but says we will have to be patient about the money we asked for; he has had some trouble and has used up all the money." The rest of the evening is spent in silence. And when they kneel down to pray, this lonely woman sends to heaven a prayer without an "Amen." Small wonder most of them are old women at the age of thirty, emaciated, tired and worn-out.

VOCABULARY

emaciated—extremely thin and underfed, as if from starvation.

A. REFLECT After reading, stop a moment to reflect about what you have learned.

1. What might it mean for the family when a woman gets a letter from her husband?

2. How are the women on the Reserves alike or different from women you know?

B. COMPARE AND CONTRAST When you compare two things, you tell how they are alike. When you contrast two things, you tell how they are different.

Use a Venn diagram to compare and contrast the men and the women in the families described in "The Widows of the Reserves."

Here, write how men and women are the same.

MEN

WOMEN

Put facts about men here.

Put facts about women here.

live in work centers

live in the Reserves

lonely

IV. WRITE

Imagine that you are writing an **article** about the women of the Reserves.

1. Use the notes from your Venn diagram.
2. Describe the women and the roles they have in their families.
3. Use the Writers' Checklist to help you revise.

The first sentence should tell what the rest of the paragraph will be about.

Here, give specific details about the women of the Reserves.

The last sentence should wrap up the description. Restate the first sentence using slightly different words.

WRITERS' CHECKLIST

COMMAS

☐ Did you use a comma between coordinate adjectives not joined by and? EXAMPLE: *The wives were sad, frightened people.*

☐ Did you use a comma to set off transition words and parenthetical expressions? EXAMPLE: *Finally, they did receive a letter.*

What things did this article make you think about?

Luis Rodriguez

Luis Rodriguez (1954–) is an internationally celebrated poet and author. He is best known for his 1993 memoir, *Always Running*, a personal account of his troubled past and later success as a poet, writer, and community activist.

Luis Rodriguez

ALWAYS RUNNING

LA
VIDA
LOCA:
GANG
DAYS
IN
L.A.

LUIS J. RODRIGUEZ

Before you read nonfiction, take a moment to walk through the selection. Notice the title and look for headings and footnotes. Examine any pictures, art, diagrams, and drawings. Get a feel for what you are about to read.

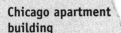

BEFORE YOU READ

Read the title and the first two paragraphs.

1. Thumb through the rest of the selection. Pay special attention to repeated names, the kinds of vocabulary words, and the photographs.

2. Then make notes on the Walk-Through below.

Chicago apartment building

"Ramiro" from *Always Running* by Luis Rodriguez

Late winter Chicago, early 1991: The once-white snow which fell in December had turned into a dark <u>scum</u>, mixed with ice-melting salt, car oil and decay. <u>Icicles</u> hung from rooftops and windowsills like the whiskers of old men.

For months, the bone-chilling "hawk" swooped down and forced everyone in the family to squeeze into a one-and-a-half bedroom apartment in a gray-stone, three-flat building in the Humboldt Park neighborhood.

VOCABULARY
scum—garbage or worthless matter.
Icicles—dagger-like spikes of ice formed by freezing or dripping water.

My Walk-Through

WHAT DID YOU LEARN ON YOUR WALK-THROUGH? AT THE TIP OF EACH SPOKE WRITE ONE FACT ABOUT "RAMIRO." ADD MORE SPOKES IF YOU NEED THEM.

set in Chicago

"Ramiro"

Choose a reading partner. Take turns reading aloud.
1. Underline information about Luis Rodriguez, and circle information about Ramiro Rodriguez.
2. In the Response Notes, write any **reactions** you have to what happens.

"Ramiro" CONTINUED

Inside tensions built up like fever as we crammed around the TV set or kitchen table, the crowding made more <u>intolerable</u> because of heaps of paper, opened file drawers and shelves packed with books that garnered every section of empty space (a sort of <u>writer's</u> <u>torture chamber</u>). The family included my third wife Trini; our child, Rubén Joaquín, born in 1988; and my 15-year-old son Ramiro (a 13-year-old daughter, Andrea, lived with her mother in East Los Angeles).

We hardly <u>ventured</u> outside. Few things were worth heaving on the layers of clothing and the coats, boots and gloves required to step out the door.

Ramiro had been placed on punishment, but not for an act of disobedience or the usual outburst of teenage anxiety. Ramiro had been on a rapidly declining roller coaster ride into the world of street-gang America, not unexpected for this neighborhood, once designated as one of the 10 poorest in the country and also known as one of the most gang-infested.

RESPONSE NOTES

EXAMPLE:

Luis = writer
Ramiro = 15 yrs. old

STOP aND THiNK

This selection makes me think about . . .

....

....

VOCABULARY
intolerable—not possible to be endured any longer.
torture chamber—place of great pain or unpleasantness.
ventured—went.

RESPONSE NOTES

Humboldt Park is a predominantly Puerto Rican community with growing numbers of Mexican immigrants and uprooted blacks and sprinklings of Ukrainians and Poles from previous generations. But along with the greater West Town area it was considered a "changing neighborhood," dotted here and there with <u>rehabs</u>, signs of <u>gentrification</u> and for many of us, <u>imminent</u> <u>displacement</u>.

Weeks before, Ramiro had received a 10-day suspension from Roberto Clemente High School, a <u>beleaguered</u> school with a good number of caring

Humboldt Park neighborhood of Chicago

<u>personnel</u>, but one which, unfortunately, was an <u>epicenter</u> of gang activity. The suspension came after a school fight which involved a war between "Insanes" and "Maniacs," two factions of the "Folks" ("Folks" are those gangs allied with the Spanish Cobras and Gangster Disciples; the "People" are gangs tied to the Latin Kings and Vice Lords, <u>symbolic</u> of the complicated structures most inner-city gangs had come to establish). There was also an "S.O.S."—a "smash-on-sight"—contract issued on Ramiro. As a result I took him out of Clemente and enrolled him in another school. He lasted less than two weeks before school officials there kicked him out. By

VOCABULARY
rehabs—short for *rehabilitation*, or buildings that have been fixed up.
gentrification—upgrading of rundown urban property by the middle class, often with the result of driving out lower income families.
imminent—about to occur.
displacement—removal from a place.
beleaguered—harassed; trouble-filled.
personnel—people employed by an organization.
epicenter—center.
symbolic—serving as a sign or symbol.

then I also had to pick him up from local jails following other fighting incidents—and once from a hospital where I watched a doctor put 11 stitches above his eye.

RESPONSE NOTES

STOP aND THiNK

Why is Ramiro in danger? Why is his father worried?

....

....

....

....

Following me, Ramiro was a second-generation gang member. My involvement was in the late 1960s and early 1970s in Los Angeles, the so-called gang capital of the country. My teen years were ones of drugs, shootings and beatings, and arrests. I was around when South Central Los Angeles gave birth to the Crips and Bloods. By the time I turned 18 years old, 25 of my friends had been killed by rival gangs, police, drugs, car crashes and suicides.

If I had barely survived all this—to emerge eventually as a journalist, publisher, critic, and poet—it

A house in Humboldt Park

appeared unlikely my own son would make it. I had to cut his blood line to the street early, before it became too late. I had to begin the long, intense struggle to save his life from the gathering storm of street violence sweeping the country—some 20 years after I sneaked out of my 'hood in the dark of night, hid out in an L.A. housing project, and removed myself from the death-fires of *La Vida Loca.*

La Vida Loca or The Crazy Life is what we called the barrio gang experience. This lifestyle originated with the Mexican *Pachuco* gangs of the 1930s and 1940s, and was later recreated with the *Cholos.* It became the main model and influence for outlaw bikers of the 1950s and 1960s, the L.A. punk/rock scene in the 1970s and 1980s, and the Crips and Bloods of the 1980s and early 1990s. As Leon Bing commented in her 1991 book *Do or Die* (HarperCollins): "It was the *cholo* homeboy who first walked the walk and talked the talk. It was the Mexican American *pachuco* who initiated the emblematic tattoos, the signing with hands, the writing of legends on walls."

VOCABULARY
barrio—Spanish word for neighborhood.
originated—began.
initiated—started.
emblematic—symbolic.

STOP AND THINK

I predict Ramiro will . . .

....

....

....

....

GATHER YOUR THOUGHTS

A. ORGANIZE Good storytellers put events in a story in an order that is easy to follow. Use this chart to recall the events in Rodriguez's story.

1.	2.	3.
4.	**5.**	**6.**

A. NARROW In "Ramiro," from *Always Running*, Rodriguez doesn't tell about every part of his life. Instead, he narrows the focus and concentrates on things that relate to Ramiro and *La Vida Loca*. Begin to focus on part of your own life to write about by filling out the graphic below.

My life in Humboldt Park

(NARROWER)
My family

(NARROWER)
My son, Ramiro

(NARROWER)
Ramiro's involvement in "La Vida Loca"

TOPIC: **RAMIRO'S INVOLVEMENT IN "LA VIDA LOCA"**

My life . . .

(NARROWER)

(NARROWER)

(NARROWER)

TOPIC:

C. FOCUS Now prepare to do some autobiographical writing of your own. Focus on the narrowed topic you came up with on the previous page. Use this "story star" to help organize the story you are going to tell.

Where?

When?

Who?

TITLE:

How did it end?

What was it all about?

IV. WRITE

Now write an **autobiographical paragraph**.

1. Stay focused on your narrowed topic and tell about the points of your star.
2. Use the Writers' Checklist to help you revise.

WRITERS' CHECKLIST

COMMAS

❏ Did you use commas in dates between the month and the year or the day and the year? EXAMPLE: *I started school on September 4, 1989.*

❏ Did you use commas to separate towns, counties, states, and districts? EXAMPLE: *My first school was in Washington, DC.*

❏ Did you use commas around an appositive, or an explanatory word or phrase? EXAMPLE: *Luis, my brother, went first.*

V. WRAP-UP

What, if anything, did you like about Luis Rodriguez's style of writing?

READERS' CHECKLIST

STYLE

- ❑ **Did you find the piece well written?**
- ❑ **Are the sentences well constructed and the words well chosen?**
- ❑ **Does the style show you how to be a better writer?**

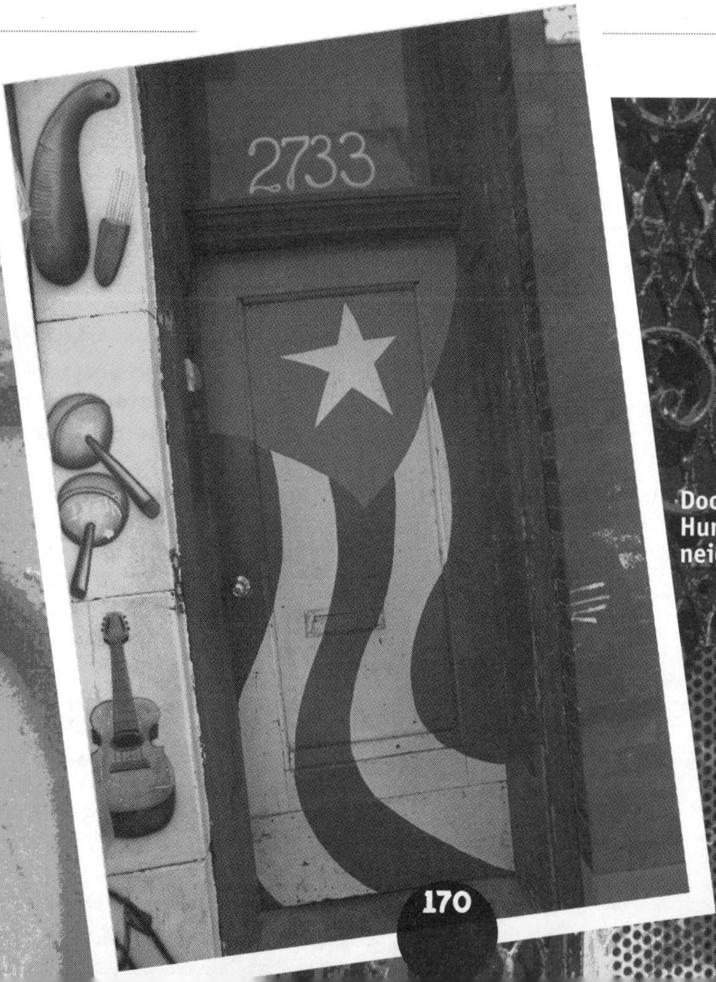

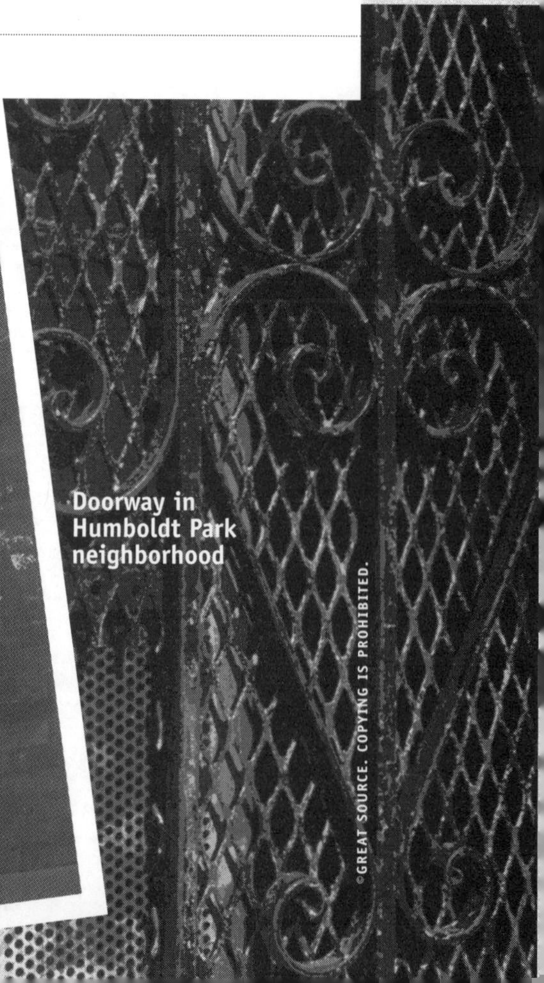

Doorway in Humboldt Park neighborhood

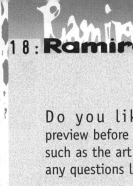

18: Ramiro CONTINUED

Do you like movie previews? Successful readers often preview before they begin reading. In a preview, look at things such as the art or photos, headings, words that stand out, and any questions listed.

BEFORE YOU READ

Review what happened in the first part of "Ramiro" on pages 162-166.

1. Next preview the second part of "Ramiro" by glancing through it quickly.

2. Make some notes on the Preview Card below.

PREVIEW CARD

WHAT DOES THE SELECTION SEEM TO BE ABOUT?

WHO SEEM TO BE THE MAIN CHARACTERS?

WHAT ARE SOME KEY VOCABULARY WORDS?

WHAT CLUES DO THE QUESTIONS IN THE "STOP" BOXES GIVE YOU ABOUT WHAT HAPPENS IN THE REST OF "RAMIRO"?

LA MANO

Take turns reading aloud from the rest of the selection.
1. When you come to a "stop" break, discuss your ideas and **predictions** about what will happen next.
2. In the Response Notes, draw or sketch some of the things that happen to help you **visualize** the action.

RESPONSE NOTES

"Ramiro" (continued) from *Always Running*
by Luis Rodriguez

One evening that winter, after Ramiro had come in late following weeks of trouble at school, I gave him an <u>ultimatum</u>. Yelling burst back and forth between the walls of our Humboldt Park flat. Two-year-old Rubén, confused and afraid, hugged my leg as the shouting erupted. In moments, Ramiro ran out of the house, entering the cold Chicago night without a jacket. I went after him, although by my mid-thirties I had gained enough weight to slow me down considerably. Still I sprinted down the <u>gangway</u> which led to a <u>debris-strewn</u> alley, filled with furniture parts and overturned trash cans. I saw Ramiro's fleeing figure, his breath rising above him in quickly-<u>dissipating</u> clouds.

EXAMPLE:

stop and clarify

Whom or what is Ramiro running from?

I followed him toward Augusta Boulevard, the main drag of the neighborhood. People yelled out of windows and doorways: "¿Qué pasa, hombre?" Others offered information on Ramiro's direction. A father or mother chasing some child down the street is not an unfamiliar sight around here.

VOCABULARY
ultimatum—final statement.
gangway—narrow passageway.
debris-strewn—filled with litter or garbage.
dissipating—disappearing.

A city like Chicago has so many places in which to hide. The gray and brown brick buildings seem to suck people in. Ramiro would make a turn and then vanish, only to pop up again. Appearing and disappearing. He flew over brick walls, scurried down another alley then veered into a building that swallowed him up and spit him out the other side.

I kept after Ramiro until, unexpectedly, I found him hiding in some bushes. He stepped out, unaware I was to the side of him.

STOP AND PREDICT

What do you predict Rodriguez will say to his son?

....

....

"Ramiro . . . come home," I gently implored, knowing if I pounced on him there would be little hope he'd come back. He sped off again.

"Leave me alone!" he yelled.

As I watched his escape, it was like looking back into a distant time, back to my own youth, when I ran and ran, when I jumped over peeling fences, fleeing *vatos locos*, the police or my own shadow in some drug-induced hysteria.

I saw Ramiro run off and then saw *my* body entering the mouth of darkness, my breath cutting the frigid flesh of night; it was my voice cracking open the winter sky.

?? STOP aND QUestion ??

What do you think Rodriguez means when he says that his voice cracked "open the winter sky"?

....

....

VOCABULARY
scurried—ran off.
veered—changed course.
hysteria—uncontrollable emotion, such as fear or panic.
frigid—extremely cold; freezing.

A. SUMMARIZE Take a moment to write what you learned from Luis Rodriguez's memoir.

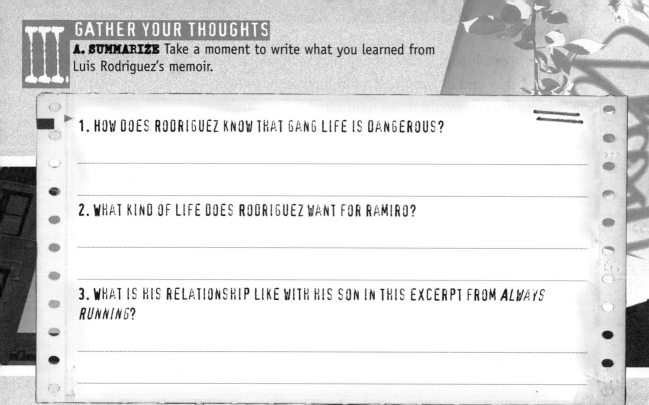

1. HOW DOES RODRIGUEZ KNOW THAT GANG LIFE IS DANGEROUS?

2. WHAT KIND OF LIFE DOES RODRIGUEZ WANT FOR RAMIRO?

3. WHAT IS HIS RELATIONSHIP LIKE WITH HIS SON IN THIS EXCERPT FROM *ALWAYS RUNNING*?

B. ORGANIZE When you prepare to write about someone you've read about, take the time to plan what you will say. Use the organizer below to help you gather your thoughts about Ramiro.

How Ramiro feels

What Ramiro does

Ramiro

How I feel about him

How his father feels about him

IV. WRITE

Write a **character description** of Ramiro.

1. Describe for someone who has not read "Ramiro" how he feels and what his situation is.

2. Begin with a topic sentence that makes a general statement about Ramiro.

3. Use the Writers' Checklist to help you revise your paragraph.

Continue your writing on the next page.

WRITERS' CHECKLIST

COMMAS

❏ **Did you use a comma to set off introductory words and phrases?**
EXAMPLE: *In the beginning, Ramiro was angry.*

❏ **Did you use a comma to set off direct quotations?** EXAMPLE: *"Ramiro, come home," I gently implored. He replied, "No! Go home!"*

Continue your writing from the previous page.

V. WRAP-UP

What things did Rodriguez's story about his son make you think about?

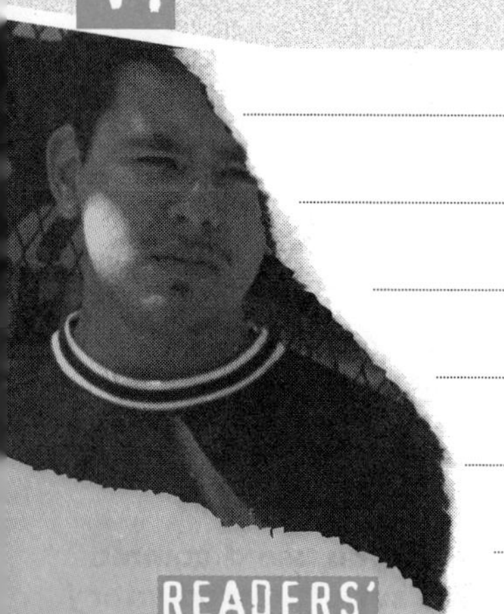

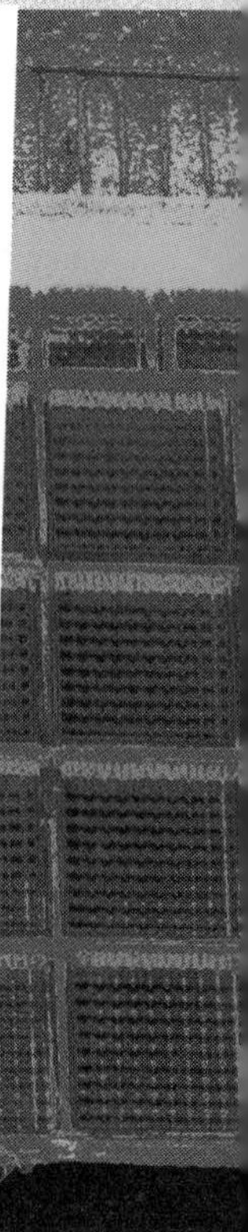

READERS' CHECKLIST

DEPTH

- ❑ **Did the reading make you think about things?**
- ❑ **Did it set off thoughts beyond the surface topic?**

"As Americans we need to take a little time to look and listen carefully to what is around us. . . ."

"Education is the key to understanding."

"My business was threatened."

". . . self-interest rides over all sorts of lines."

Zora Neale Hurston

If you find out a little about a story or article before you read, it will help you figure out where a selection is headed.

BEFORE YOU READ

Read each of these statements. Place a check in the category that tells how you feel about the statement.

Anticipation Guide

AGREE	DISAGREE	NEUTRAL	
			1. Under the Constitution of the United States, all people are equal.
			2. You should risk your job or your money to protect people whom you care about.
			3. People are more interested in helping themselves than in helping other people, even if the people are just like they are.
			4. All people are equally welcome in restaurants, stores, barber shops, and so on.

1. Have these ideas always been true in the United States? Use a different color pen and place marks to show whether you agree or disagree that these ideas were <u>always</u> true.
2. Share your answers with a partner. Explain why you reacted to each statement as you did. Did your answers change as you thought about these statements today and in the past?
3. Now make a prediction with your partner.

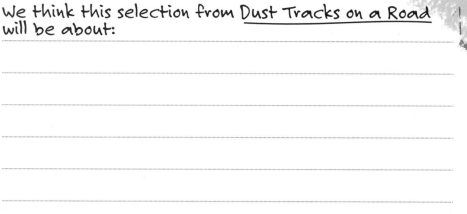

We think this selection from <u>Dust Tracks on a Road</u> will be about:

_____

_____

_____

_____

_____

_____

II. READ

Read the selection at your own pace.

1. Underline parts where you see a conflict between people or ideas.

2. In the Response Notes, write any **questions** you have or want to ask the author.

Response Notes

"Refusing Service" from *Dust Tracks on a Road* by Zora Neale Hurston

An incident happened that made me realize how <u>theories</u> go by the board when a person's livelihood is threatened. A man, a Negro, came into the shop one afternoon and sank down in Banks's chair. Banks was the manager and had the first chair by the door. It was so surprising that for a minute Banks just looked at him and never said a word. Finally, he found his tongue and asked, "What do you want?"

"Hair-cut and shave," the man said <u>belligerently</u>.

EXAMPLE:
When did this take place? Where?

"But you can't get no hair-cut and shave here. Mr. Robinson has a fine shop for Negroes on U Street near Fifteenth," Banks told him.

"I know it, but I want one here. The Constitution of the United States—"

But by that time, Banks had him by the arm. Not roughly, but he was helping him out of his chair, nevertheless.

"I don't know how to cut your hair," Banks objected. "I was trained on straight hair. Nobody in here knows how."

"Oh, don't hand me that stuff!" the <u>crusader</u> <u>snarled</u>. "Don't be such an Uncle Tom."

"Run on, fellow. You can't get waited on in here."

"I'll stay right here until I do. I know my rights. Things like this have got to be broken up. I'll get waited on all right, or <u>sue</u> the place."

VOCABULARY

theories—ideas, beliefs, or assumptions.
belligerently—angrily, in a hostile way as if eager to fight.
crusader—someone who works vigorously for a cause or against an abuse.
snarled—spoke angrily.
sue—go to court to get justice for a wrong done.

BARBER

179

"Go ahead and sue," Banks retorted. "Go on uptown, and get your hair cut, man. Don't be so hardheaded for nothing."

"I'm getting waited on right here!"

"You're next, Mr. Powell," Banks said to a waiting customer. "Sorry, mister, but you better go on uptown."

Story Frame

THIS STORY
TAKES PLACE ············▶

············▶ ARE CHARACTERS
IN THE STORY

A PROBLEM
HAPPENS WHEN ············▶

"But I have a right to be waited on wherever I please," the Negro said, and started towards Updyke's chair which was being emptied. Updyke whirled his chair around so that he could not sit down and stepped in front of it. "Don't you touch *my* chair!" Updyke glared. "Go on about your business."

But instead of going, he made to get into the chair by force.

"Don't argue with him! Throw him out of here!" somebody in the back cried. And in a minute, barbers, customers all lathered and hair half cut, and porters, were all helping to throw the Negro out.

The rush carried him way out into the middle of G Street and flung him down. He tried to lie there and be a martyr, but the roar of oncoming cars made him jump up and scurry off. We never heard any more about it. I did not participate in the mêlée, but I wanted him thrown out, too. My business was threatened.

VOCABULARY
whirled—turned or spun quickly.
lathered—covered with a foam or soap in preparation for a shave.
porters—attendants.
martyr—one who chooses to suffer injury or death rather than to give up one's cause.
scurry—run off with light, quick steps.
mêlée—fight, disturbance, or scuffle.

"Refusing Service" continued

It was only that night in bed that I analyzed the whole thing and realized that I was giving sanction to Jim Crow, which theoretically, I was supposed to resist. But here were ten Negro barbers, three porters and two manicurists all stirred up at the threat of our living through loss of patronage. Nobody thought it out at the moment. It was an instinctive thing. That was the first time it was called to my attention that self-interest rides over all sorts of lines. I have seen the same thing happen hundreds of times since, and now I understand it. One sees it breaking over racial, national, religious and class lines. Anglo-Saxon against Anglo-Saxon, Jew against Jew, Negro against Negro, and all sorts of combinations of the three against other combinations of the three. Offhand, you might say that we fifteen Negroes should have felt the racial thing and served him. He was one of us. Perhaps it would have been a beautiful thing if Banks had turned to the shop crowded with customers and announced that this man was going to be served like everybody else even at the risk of losing their patronage, with all of the other employees lined up in the center of the floor shouting, "So say we all!" It would have been a stirring gesture, and made the headlines for a day. Then we could all have gone home to our unpaid rents and bills and things like that. I could leave school and begin my wanderings again. The "militant" Negro who would

VOCABULARY

sanction—support or approval of an action, making it valid.
Jim Crow—name given to laws discriminating against African Americans.
theoretically—in theory, or as an idea.
manicurists—people who shape, polish, and trim fingernails.
patronage—business.
militant—fighting or warring; one having a combative character.

have been the cause of it all, would have perched on the smuddled-up wreck of things and crowed. Nobody ever found out who or what he was. Perhaps he did what he did on the spur of the moment, not realizing that serving him would have ruined Mr. Robinson, another Negro who had got what he had the hard way. For not only would the G Street shop have been forced to close, but the F Street shop and all of his other six downtown shops. Wrecking George Robinson like that on a "race" angle would have been <u>ironic</u> tragedy. He always helped out any Negro who was trying to do anything progressive as far as he was able. He had no education himself, but he was for it. He would give any Howard University student a job in his shops if they could qualify, even if it was only a few hours a week.

Story Frame

HOW DOES THE INCIDENT END?

So I do not know what was the ultimate right in this case. I do know how I felt at the time. There is always something fiendish and loathsome about a person who threatens to deprive you of your way of making a living. That is just human-like, I reckon.

VOCABULARY

ironic—made the opposite of what it really was because of the difference between what is expected and what actually occurs.

Story Frame

WHY DO YOU THINK HURSTON TELLS THIS STORY?

GATHER YOUR THOUGHTS

A. RESTATE AN OPINION The narrator of this story has an opinion: *Self-interest is often more important than any other loyalties.* Restate this opinion in *your* own words:

FACT can be proven true or false.

OPINION is someone's belief or idea.

B. SUPPORT AN OPINION A good writer supports opinions with facts. What facts does the narrator share to prove her opinion? List them here:

Self-interest is often more important than any other loyalties.

FACT

FACT

FACT

C. FORM AN OPINION Now write an opinion of your own.

1. What do you think this selection tells about people and the way they treat one another? Complete the sentence below.

In my opinion, "Refusing Service" shows

2. Look through the selection again, paying attention to passages that relate to the sentence you just wrote. List some ideas from the selection that support your opinion.

FACT

FACT

FACT

FACT

WRITE

Write an **opinion paragraph**. Explain what "Refusing Service" says about how people treat one another.

1. State your opinion in the first sentence.
2. Use your list of facts to support your opinion.
3. Use the Writers' Checklist to help you revise.

The first sentence states your opinion.

Use facts from your list here.

Sum up your arguments here.

WRITERS' CHECKLIST

CAPITALIZATION

❑ **Did you capitalize the first word of every sentence** including the first word of a direct quotation that is a complete sentence? EXAMPLE: *"I don't know how to cut your hair," Banks observed. "I was trained on straight hair. Nobody in here knows how."*

❑ **Did you remember not to capitalize the first word of an indirect quotation?** An indirect quotation does not tell the speaker's exact words. EXAMPLE: *The narrator says that she wondered if she should have helped the man in the shop.*

❑ **Did you remember always to capitalize the pronoun I** no matter where it appears in a sentence? EXAMPLE: *After I read the story, I wondered what I would do in that same situation.*

V. WRAP-UP

What did you learn about people and how they relate to each other?

_____

_____

_____

_____

_____

_____

_____

_____

_____

_____

20: Time to Look and Listen

Have you ever looked ahead in a book to see how long it is or how it ends? That's a way of skimming. Readers often skim before they read to get a better idea of what's coming up.

I. BEFORE YOU READ

Skimming means "to glide or pass quickly and lightly over." As a reader, that's what you can do before reading textbooks or nonfiction articles. Here's what to look for:

1. Look for key words and phrases that keep appearing.

2. Notice names of people and places.

3. Think of skimming as a kind of treasure hunt. Use the space below to help you gather and record information as you skim.

Skimming

PLACES

PEOPLE

KEY WORDS AND PHRASES

II. READ
Read the whole essay. Take as much time as you need.
1. React to anything that strikes you.
2. Use the Response Notes to jot down your own views about what happens.

Response Notes

"Time to Look and Listen" by Magdoline Asfahani

I love my country as many who have been here for generations cannot. Perhaps that's because I'm the child of immigrants, raised with a <u>conscious</u> respect for America that many people take for granted. My parents chose this country because it offered them a new life, freedom and possibilities. But I learned at a young age that the country we loved so much did not feel the same way about us.

<u>Discrimination</u> is not unique to America. It occurs in any country that allows immigration. Anyone who is unlike the majority is looked at a little <u>suspiciously</u>, dealt with a little differently. The fact that I wasn't part of the majority never occurred to me. I knew that I was an Arab and a Muslim. This meant nothing to me. At school I stood up to say the Pledge of Allegiance every day. These things did not seem <u>incompatible</u> at all. Then everything changed for me, suddenly and permanently, in 1985. I was only in seventh grade, but that was the beginning of my political education.

That year a TWA plane originating in Athens was <u>diverted</u> to Beirut. Two years earlier the U.S. Marine <u>barracks</u> in Beirut had been bombed. That seemed to start a chain of events that would forever link Arabs with <u>terrorism</u>. After the hijacking, I faced classmates

EXAMPLE:
I never think about what the words in the Pledge mean. Does anybody?

VOCABULARY
conscious—having an awareness of something.
Discrimination—treatment or consideration based on a class or category rather than on individual merit.
suspiciously—distrustfully.
incompatible—unable to be blend in or fit together.
diverted—turned aside from a course or direction.
barracks—housing for military personnel.
terrorism—unlawful or threatened use of force or violence to make societies or governments do something, often for political or religious reasons.

"**Time to Look and Listen**" continued

who taunted me with cruel names, attacking my heritage and my religion. I became an outcast and had to apologize for myself constantly.

After a while, I tried to forget my heritage. No matter what race, religion or ethnicity, a child who is attacked often retreats. I was the only Arab I knew of in my class, so I had no one in my peer group as an ally. No matter what my parents tried to tell me about my proud cultural history, I would ignore it. My classmates told me I came from an uncivilized, brutal place, that Arabs were by nature anti-American, and I believed them. They did not know the hours my parents spent studying, working, trying to preserve part of their old lives while embracing, willingly, the new.

Begin a graphic organizer. Asfahani has described a problem. Write the problem in the organizer.

PROBLEM

ISSUE   ISSUE   ISSUE

SOLUTION

PROBLEM

I tried to forget the Arabic I knew, because if I didn't I'd be forever linked to murderers. I stopped inviting friends over for dinner, because I thought the food we ate was "weird." I lied about where my parents had come from. Their accents (although they spoke English perfectly) humiliated me. Though Islam is a major

VOCABULARY
heritage—something passed down from earlier generations.
ethnicity—having a common racial, national, religious, or cultural heritage.
retreats—withdraws.
peer—one who has equal standing with another, especially in rank, class, or age.
uncivilized—barbaric; lacking in courtesy or manners.

monotheistic religion with many similarities to
Judaism and Christianity, there were no holidays near
Chanukah or Christmas, nothing to tie me to the
"Judeo-Christian" tradition. I felt more excluded. I
slowly began to turn into someone without a past.

Civil war was raging in Lebanon, and all that
Americans saw of that country was destruction and
violence. Every other movie seemed to feature Arab
terrorists. The most common questions I was asked
were if I had ever ridden a camel or if my family lived
in tents. I felt burdened with responsibility. Why should
an adolescent be asked questions like "Is it true you
hate Jews and you want Israel destroyed?" I didn't hate
anybody. My parents had never said anything even
alluding to such sentiments. I was confused and hurt.

Asfahani describes several issues surrounding the problem.
Describe two other issues related to the problem. Write an issue
in each of the boxes.

ISSUE	ISSUE	ISSUE
Asfahani feels alone. She is so different from her classmates that she feels ashamed.		

VOCABULARY
monotheistic—believing there is only one god.
Chanukah—another spelling of Hanukkah, an eight-day Jewish festival and celebration.

As I grew older and began to form my own opinions, my embarrassment lessened and my anger grew. The turning point came in high school. My grandmother had become very ill, and it was necessary for me to leave school a few days before Christmas vacation. My chemistry teacher was very sympathetic until I said I was going to the Middle East. "Don't come back in a body bag," he said cheerfully. The class laughed. Suddenly, those years of watching movies that mocked me and listening to others who knew nothing about Arabs and Muslims except what they saw on television seemed like a bad dream. I knew then that I would never be silent again.

I've tried to reclaim those lost years. I realize now that I come from a culture that has a rich history. The Arab world is a medley of people of different religions; not every Arab is a Muslim, and vice versa. The Arabs brought tremendous advances in the sciences and mathematics, as well as creating a literary tradition that has never been surpassed. The language itself is flexible and beautiful, with nuances and shades of meaning unparalleled in any language. Though many find it hard to believe, Islam has made progress in women's rights. There is a specific provision in the Koran that permits women to own property and ensures that their inheritance is protected—although recent events have shown that interpretation of these laws can vary.

VOCABULARY

medley—mix of things that do not normally belong together.
nuances—shades of expression and feeling.
unparalleled—unequaled; matchless.
provision—statement that makes a condition.
Koran—sacred book of the Muslims, said to have the revelations of the prophet Mohammed.

My youngest brother, who is 12, is now at the crossroads I faced. When initial reports of the Oklahoma City bombing pointed to "Arab-looking individuals" as the culprits, he came home from school crying. "Mom, why do Muslims kill people? Why are the Arabs so bad?" She was angry and brokenhearted, but tried to handle the situation in the best way possible: through education. She went to his class, armed with Arabic music, pictures, traditional dress and cookies. She brought a chapter of the social-studies book to life, and the children asked intelligent, thoughtful questions, even after the class was over. Some even asked if she was coming back. When my brother came home, he was excited and proud instead of ashamed.

I only recently told my mother about my past experience. Maybe if I had told her then, I would have been better equipped to deal with the thoughtless teasing. But, fortunately, the world is changing. Although discrimination and stereotyping still exist, many people are trying to lessen and end it. Teachers, schools and the media are showing greater sensitivity to cultural issues. However, there is still much that needs to be done, not for the sake of any particular ethnic or cultural group but for the sake of our country.

VOCABULARY

culprits—persons guilty of a crime or a fault.
stereotyping—oversimplifying an idea about a person, group, or thought.

The America that I love is one that values freedom and the differences of its people. Education is the key to understanding. As Americans we need to take a little time to look and listen carefully to what is around us and not rush to judgment without knowing all the facts. And we must never be ashamed of our pasts. It is our collective differences that unite us and make us unique as a nation. It's what determines our present and our future.

Asfahani gives her ideas for solving the problem. Restate the solution in your own words.

SOLUTION

GATHER YOUR THOUGHTS

A. LOOK CLOSELY Asfahani has an opinion that she wants her readers to believe. Her opinion is:

> ➤ *As Americans, we need to take a little time to look and listen carefully to what is around us and not rush to judgment without knowing all the facts.*

How does she support this opinion or help you to believe that this opinion is true?

1. Go back to the article. Circle any sentences that support her opinion.

2. Jot down any notes or ideas you have about Asfahani's statements and what she does to support her opinion.

B. DEVELOP AN OPINION Now write an opinion of your own. What do you think is the best way to get rid of prejudice or unfair treatment of others? Write your own opinion here:

The best way to get rid of prejudice is

C. SUPPORT THE OPINION List at least 2 or 3 ideas that support your opinion. Don't worry about writing complete sentences or having "perfect" ideas. Just list whatever comes to mind.

WRITE

Now write an **article of opinion**. Your purpose should be to suggest a way to fight prejudice.

1. Give your opinion in the opening sentence.
2. Use the ideas you listed to support your opinion persuasively.
3. Use the Writers' Checklist to revise your article.

In my opinion, the best way to fight prejudice is

WRITERS' CHECKLIST

APOSTROPHES

❏ **Did you use apostrophes correctly in writing the possessive form of singular nouns? To show ownership, add an 's to singular nouns.** EXAMPLES: *my brother's computer, Chris's belief, a magazine's headline*

❏ **Did you use apostrophes correctly in writing the possessive form of plural nouns? Add only an apostrophe to plural nouns that end in s.** EXAMPLES: *all of the girls' books, the many students' letters* **Add 's to plural nouns that do not end in s.** EXAMPLE: *children's homework, people's prejudice*

V. WRAP-UP

In your own words, what point was the writer trying to make?

The Holocaust rem
one of the darkes
periods in recent his
Between 1933 and
the Nazi governmen
Germany murdered
millions of innocent
people because of t
race, religion, or be
As the main targets
the Nazis, Jews suff
drastic losses. By th
end of World War II
1945, two out of
every three Europea
Jews had been
killed.

21: A Soldier's Letter Home

What was the last letter you wrote like? What was it about? As readers, we use everything we have ever learned or done. Before reading this letter, consider what you know about the subject. One tool that can help is a K-W-L chart.

BEFORE YOU READ

Read the title and first paragraph of this part of a soldier's letter to his wife.
1. Think about what you already know about this subject and what you want to find out.
2. Complete the K and W parts of the chart below.

"A Soldier's Letter Home" by Delbert Cooper

5/6/45
Austria

My dearest Joan:

...Yesterday I was to a <u>concentration camp</u>. From what I saw with my own eyes, everything I ever heard about those places is absolutely true.

VOCABULARY
concentration camp—prison camp where prisoners of war or members of minority groups are held.

K-W-L CHART

World War II: Concentration Camps

K WHAT I KNOW
+ +

W WHAT I WANT TO KNOW
+ +

L WHAT I HAVE LEARNED
+ +

READ

Now read the rest of the letter.
1. Circle or highlight information that is new to you.
2. Put a question mark in the margin if you come across something you don't understand or have **questions** about.

"A Soldier's Letter Home" CONTINUED

Here is how I happened to be there and a little about it. The report came to us of this concentration camp being 5 kilometers down the road. It so happened that we had captured a whole German supply train the night before. So, 4 of us loaded up a truck with food & took it down. I'm going to tell you now I never want to see a sight again as we saw when we pulled in there. 1400 starving diseased, stinking people. It was terrible. Most of them were Jews that Hitler had put away for safekeeping. Some of them had been in camps for as long as 8 years. So help me, I cannot see how they stood it. No longer were most of them people. They were nothing but things that were once human beings. As we pulled off of the highway into the camp we had to shove them off of the truck. We had the first food that had been taken in there for a month. The people for the most part were dirty walking skeletons. Some were too weak to walk. They had had nothing to eat for so long. Some of them were still lying around dead where they had fallen. Others would fall as they tried to keep up with the truck. We were moving slow as we didn't want to run over anyone. We stopped to start to unload the food and then we really had a time. We tried & tried to keep them from crowding us so we could unload but they were just about beyond reasoning. Finally about four of them who spoke English started getting a little order for us. Even then we had to get off the truck & start shoving them out of the road. You could stand right in front of them & wave your arms for them to move over & they would just stand there, look right in your face and cry like a baby. It

RESPONSE NOTES

EXAMPLE:

What did he think it would be like? How had he known anything about the camps?

VOCABULARY

kilometers—units of length equal to 1,000 meters (about 2/3 of a mile).
skeletons—the bones in the body supporting the muscles and organs. Here the writer uses the word *skeleton* as a metaphor to mean the prisoners were abnormally thin.

was really a <u>pathetic</u> scene. Finally we took out our guns & pointed them in their faces, but they still stood there and <u>bawled</u>. They were past being afraid of even a gun.

We fired a few shots up in the air & still we couldn't clear them. They just couldn't believe that we had food for everyone. We pulled on farther back in to the camp after about half an hour, & the fellows who spoke English started getting some order.

stop and think

Why are the prisoners crying?

Why do they refuse to move away from the truck?

Then we started to unload. We picked out about 15 to help us. How those skinny fellows ever lifted those boxes is beyond me. They were heavy for us to lift. But they got them off. While we were standing outside the truck, any number of them came up & touched us, as if they couldn't believe we were actually there. Some of them would try to kiss us even. (They must have been bad off.) Some of them would come up, grab you around the neck, & cry on your shoulder. Others would just look & cry. Some of them would throw their arms up in the air & pray. They were mostly the ones who were too weak to stand. I recall one woman who could only cry & point at her mouth. One fellow must have felt that he should give me something. As he had nothing to give of value, he gave me his little yellow star that <u>designates</u> a Jew. I'll send it to you in another letter. All of them wanted

VOCABULARY
pathetic—pitiful.
bawled—wept loudly.
designates—points out; indicates.

"A Soldier's Letter Home" CONTINUED

American cigarettes. I had given all of mine but 4 away on the road coming to the camp, so I halved the four so that eight of them could at least get a few puffs. Finally everything was unloaded. As the major who went with us couldn't get much order he left everything up to us 4 enlisted men. I estimated we had 2400 cans of <u>chow</u> aboard, so explained to one of the fellows to put two persons to a can. You see the condition these people were in—too much food all at once would probably have killed them. The cans were about the size of a regular can of peaches, so that was plenty for a starter. Someone, don't know who, had slipped 500 eggs aboard. I took one of the guys & told him to start with the children & give them one egg apiece & if he had any left over to give them to the women. The men, if you could call them that, could eat the meat. He told us people were dying at the average rate of 150 per day at this camp. They just stack them up in a pile if they died in the <u>barracks</u>. If they died outside they left them there. I know, I saw them.

stop and think

How does the soldier feel as he looks at the prisoners?

....

....

There were 4 barracks for 1400 people. Room space was 1 yard per person. Just enough room to sit down . . .

You see they had to stay off the roads so our supplies could keep rolling on. That was another thing we had to explain to them. Those that could walk wanted to travel & you can imagine how that would have been. The young people who were in this camp will probably never get over it. They will be <u>stunted</u> for life. You may see

VOCABULARY
chow—slang for "food."
barracks—buildings for soldiers to live in.
stunted—hindered; slowed down normal growth or development.

RESPONSE NOTES

pictures of this back home as they put a call through for photographers to go there. Don't know whether they went or not as after we left we didn't go back. Instead, we got a better idea. Why truck the food in there when the tracks ran close by and we had a whole train of supplies. Also an engine with steam up and an Austrian engineer. So we moved the whole damned trainload down close to the camp. Enough food & other articles there to last them till they were strong enough to go on their way.

There are two things about all this that I want to tell you.

1. I never again want to see anything like that happen to anyone.

2. I wish 130 million American people could have been standing in my shoes.

You know, that SS man I captured later in the day never came so near to dying in his life. I pointed my pistol right against his head, but I just couldn't shoot him down in cold blood. Lost my nerve when I started squeezing the trigger. Too much like murder. If he would only have put up the littlest resistance he would now be a dead man.

VOCABULARY
SS man—the "SS" refers to a select military unit of the Nazis who were assigned to security assignments, such as guarding concentration camps.
resistance—opposition; attempt to fight back or get away.

stop and think

Why does the soldier wish that "130 million American people" had seen what he saw?

Why does he want to shoot the SS man? What stops him?

GATHER YOUR THOUGHTS

A. RECORD Return to the K-W-L Chart on page 198. Record in the L space what you have learned by reading the letter.

B. CLUSTER Complete this cluster on concentration camps. Make the cluster as big as you can.

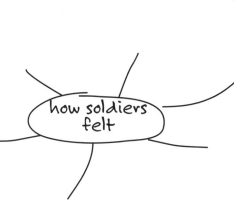

concentration camps

how soldiers felt

people who were in them

C. UNDERSTAND Most letters have a few basic parts. Look back at the letter and answer these questions.

1. What date is the letter written? (The date comes first.)

2. What is the name of the person being sent the letter? (This is called the salutation, or greeting.)

3. What 2 or 3 things did Cooper want to tell about in his letter? (This is called the body of the letter.)

4. Letters often end with a closing--such as **Sincerely** or **Yours Truly,** and then a signature. For instance, Cooper's letter ends with "Love, Del."

IV. WRITE

Write a **letter** back to this young soldier.

1. Respond to his wish that all Americans "could have been standing in my shoes." Explain to him how his letter made you feel.
2. Use the Writers' Checklist to help you revise.

date

greeting

body

WRITERS' CHECKLIST

SUBJECT-VERB AGREEMENT

☐ Did you use a plural verb in sentences with compound subjects joined by *and*? EXAMPLE: *Prejudice and hatred are destrctive.* If the parts of the subject belong to one unit, use a singular verb. EXAMPLE: *Fish and chips is on the menu.*

☐ In sentences with compound subjects joined by *or* or *nor*, did you make the verb agree with the subject closest to it? EXAMPLES: *Neiher my friends nor I know what happened. The soldiers or the reporter is going to call us.*

closing

signature

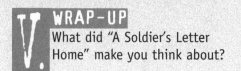

V. WRAP-UP
What did "A Soldier's Letter Home" make you think about?

READERS' CHECKLIST
DEPTH
☐ Did the reading make you think about things?
☐ Did it set off thoughts beyond the surface topic?

Good-bye

A photo can be read just like a sentence. Have you ever tried it? A picture walk is one way you can connect to a selection. Before you read, look carefully at all pictures and captions. What clues do they give you about what the writing will be about?

BEFORE YOU READ

Look at the photos and captions carefully.
1. Make a prediction about the selection's content.
2. Jot down questions and reactions you have.

PICTURE WALK

1. I PREDICT THAT THIS SELECTION WILL BE ABOUT:

Nazis rounding up Jews

Jews gathered up before being sent to concentration camps

2. I HAVE THESE QUESTIONS ABOUT THE PICTURES AND THEIR CAPTIONS:

Polish women being led to their execution

3. THESE PICTURES REMIND ME OF:

READ

Read "Good-bye," a part of Gerta Weismann Klein's memoirs.

1. As you read, **predict** what you think will happen next. Your predictions will make the reading more interesting.
2. Use the Response Notes space to **clarify** anything that seems important.

"Good-bye" from *All But My Life*
by Gerta Weismann Klein

In the morning we did not talk about the train that was to leave a few hours hence. Silently we sat at the table. Then Papa picked up his Bible and started to read. Mama and I just sat looking at him. Then all of a sudden Papa looked up and asked Mama where my skiing shoes were.

"Why?" I asked, baffled.

"I want you to wear them tomorrow when you go to Wadowitz."

"But Papa, skiing shoes in June?"

He said steadily: "I want you to wear them tomorrow."

"Yes, Papa, I will," I said in a small voice.

I wonder why Papa insisted; how could he possibly have known? Those shoes played a <u>vital</u> part in saving my life. They were sturdy and strong, and when three years later they were taken off my frozen feet they were good still. . . .

> EXAMPLE:
> Klein looks ahead and interrupts the story of the good-byes.

When it came time to leave, Papa and Mama <u>embraced</u>. Then Papa put his hands on my head in benediction, as he had done for Arthur. His hands trembled. He held me a while, then lifted my chin up and looked into my eyes. We were both weeping.

Children in concentration camp

VOCABULARY
vital—essential; very important.
embraced—hugged.

RESPONSE NOTES

"My child," he managed. It was a question and a promise. I understood. I threw myself wildly into his embrace, clinging to him in <u>desperation</u> for the last time. I gave him my most sacred vow: "Yes, Papa." We had always understood each other, but never better than in that last hour.

STOP AND PREDICT

What do you predict will happen to Gerta's father?

What do you predict will happen to Gerta?

And so we went to the station, across the <u>meadow</u>, taking the longer way, trying to be together as long as possible. A crowd was already <u>assembled</u>. Papa was asked for his <u>identification</u>. We went out onto the platform with him. The train would leave in a few minutes. People were saying their heartbreaking good-byes.

Papa entered the last car and went to the open platform at the rear to see us as long as possible. There he stood in his good gray suit, his only one, his shoulders sloping, his hair steel gray in the sun, on his breast the yellow star and black word.

There he stood, already beyond my reach, my father, the center of my life, just labeled JEW.

A shrill whistle blew through the peaceful afternoon. Like a puppet a <u>conductor</u> lifted a little red flag. Chug-chug-chug—puffs of smoke rose. The train began

VOCABULARY
desperation—the loss of all hope.
meadow—grassy field or pasture.
assembled—gathered.
identification—official papers stating a name and address.
conductor—person in charge of a railroad car, train, or bus.

"Good·bye" CONTINUED

to creep away. Papa's eyes were fixed upon us. He did not move. He did not wave. He did not call farewell. Unseen hands were moving him farther and farther away from us.

We watched until the train was out of sight. I never saw my father again.

Jews forced from homes in Poland

Only after several moments did I become conscious of the fact that Mama was with me. She took my hand like that of a baby and we started to walk toward the ghetto. I didn't once look at her. Only after a while did I realize that she too was weeping.

That night she fixed me something to eat and I ate to please her. She asked me to sleep with her in Papa's bed. I did so reluctantly. I was half asleep when I felt her arms around me, clinging to me in desperation. All my life I shall be sorry that I did not feel more tender that night. When Mama needed me most I wanted to be alone. I pulled away like a wounded animal that wants to lick its wounds in peace. Finally I fell asleep—on a pillow soaked with my mother's tears.

We rose early. While I put on my skiing boots Mama made me a cup of cocoa—the precious cocoa which she had saved for almost three years for a special occasion.

"Aren't you eating, Mama?" I asked.

"It's Monday," she answered. Mama had fasted every Monday for half a day since Arthur had left.

VOCABULARY
ghetto—walled part of a city where Jews were forced to live.
reluctantly—unwillingly; hesitantly.

German soldiers forcing Jews into a ghetto in Poland

209

RESPONSE NOTES

"But today," I said, "you should eat something."

"Today especially not," she answered from the window, holding the ivory-bound prayer book she had carried as a bride. She prayed and watched me—and I watched her. The <u>chives</u> were uprooted on the window sill. Yesterday we had taken out the few remaining jewels, sewed some into Papa's jacket, Mama's <u>corset</u>, my coat.

A shrill whistle blew through the ghetto. It was time to leave.

STOP AND PREDICT

Where do you think Gerta and her mother are going? Will they be able to stay together?

When we had made our way downstairs we saw the woman with the lovely complexion, Miss Pilzer, screaming and begging to be allowed to go with her mother. The dying old woman was thrown on a truck meant for the aged and ill. Here the <u>SS man</u> kicked her and she screamed. He kicked her again.

On the same truck were Mr. Köllander, the man with paralyzed legs, and the mother with her little girls. The twins were smiling; unaware of what was happening, they were busy catching the raindrops. An <u>epileptic</u> woman was put on the truck; her dog jumped after her. The SS man kicked him away, but the dog kept on trying

Carrying bodies for burial

VOCABULARY

chives—mild, onion-flavored plants used to season food.
corset—women's undergarment used to shape the waistline.
SS man—the "SS" refers to a select military unit of the Nazis.
epileptic—person who has the disease of epilepsy, which sometimes results in seizures and loss of control.

"Good-bye" CONTINUED

to get in the truck. To our horror, the SS man pulled his gun and shot the dog. I looked toward Mama. I wanted to run to her. I wanted to be held by her—to be comforted. Now it was too late.

Leaving the <u>invalids</u> behind, we assembled in a field in a suburb of Bielitz called Lärchenfeld. Here we were left in the rain to wait. After about four hours the SS men finally came in a shiny black car, their high boots

Jews rounded up and being sent to camps

polished to perfection. A table was set up and covered with a cloth—a tablecloth in the rain!—and at that table they checked the lists of the people present.

We had all assembled.

Why? Why did we walk like meek sheep to the <u>slaughterhouse</u>? Why did we not fight back? What had we to lose? Nothing but our lives. Why did we not run away and hide? We might have had a chance to survive. Why did we walk deliberately and obediently into their <u>clutches</u>?

I know why. Because we had faith in humanity. Because we did not really think that human beings were capable of committing such crimes.

It cleared up and then it rained again. I was tired and hungry, hot and cold, and still we stood at attention, losing track of time.

Finally, certain trucks were loaded and driven off amid crying and screaming. Mama kept looking into my eyes. Her courage gave me strength. Those of us who remained were lined up in rows of four and ordered to march to the station. Instead of marching us across the

VOCABULARY
invalids—people suffering from an illness.
slaughterhouse—place where animals are butchered.
clutches—control; power.

meadow directly to the station, we were marched all around town. Oh God, I asked, I prayed, oh God, are they going to do to us what they did to Erika's mother? Will we dig our own grave? Oh God, no, no, NO! Don't let it happen—don't! I am afraid. I don't want to die. Don't hurt Mama. Don't—

I saw Bielitz, my dear childhood town. Here and there from behind a curtain a familiar face looked out. We kept on marching. People went marketing. Guards beat stragglers with rubber truncheons. Oh God, I prayed, don't let it happen!

Someone pushed a baby carriage. Workmen were repairing a street. On the butcher shop they were painting a new sign. We were marching. A dry goods store was decorating its show window. We had bought the flowered fabric for my dress there, but it was not colorfast. Oh God, don't let it happen, don't, I prayed, don't! At the movie theater they were putting up a sign announcing a new feature—and we were marching.

I noticed Mama grow pale. She was gripping her suitcase tightly. I jerked it out of her hand.

"You hurt my hand," she said in a whisper.

Finally we approached the railroad station on the opposite side of town. Beyond the station were open meadows where the annual circus set up its tents. There we waited again.

STOP AND PREDICT

What do you guess will happen at the railroad station?

_____

_____

From mouth to mouth the news traveled: "Merin!" Merin was here. The king of the Jews, as he was called,

VOCABULARY
colorfast—fabric with color that will not run or fade.
annual—yearly.

"Good-bye" CONTINUED

had arrived. His headquarters had been at Sosnowitz where there were the biggest Jewish <u>congregation</u>, the largest factories and shops in which Jews worked.

Nazis marching Jews past their burning homes

Customarily the Nazis established someone such as Merin as head of Jewish communities and gave him the job of <u>liquidating</u> them. It was said that Merin lived in luxury, that he had visited <u>Goebbels</u>, that he was the only Jew to own a car, that he was <u>indescribably</u> wealthy. I imagine these things were true. Certainly he was master of life and death.

I looked at him now. He was short, perhaps a bit over five feet, pale and thin; he had watery eyes, dull brown hair, and he was clad in a brown raincoat. He talked in a <u>hoarse</u> whisper. He pulled a bottle of <u>schnapps</u> from his pocket, drank first and then handed it to the SS men about him. They drank after him. I saw it all and marveled. Yes, he was all right for them, he was their kind.

"I am glad you took the suitcase," Mama said very quietly. We were no longer standing at attention. "I would have fainted," she continued.

"Why didn't you throw it away?"

Her voice was without tone as she answered, "Arthur's picture is in it."

Merin was walking in our direction. Mama prompted me, "Go ask him if we are going to Wadowitz."

VOCABULARY

congregation—group of people who gather together.
liquidating—killing.
Goebbels—major leader in Nazi government and member of Hitler's close circle.
indescribably—unbelievably; extremely.
hoarse—rough or hard sounding.
schnapps—a kind of clear, dry liquor common in Germany.

I asked him in Polish—it was known that his German was very poor.

He looked at me, his eyes without expression.

"Are you crazy?" was his hoarse reply.

Mama asked me what he had said, but I had no time to answer, for "All march down this way" came the command.

In our clenched fists we held our working cards from the shop, those sacred cards that we thought meant security. As we marched along in pairs we heard cries and screams ahead of us. Mama and I held hands tightly. A cane hit our hands. They unclasped. The cane pointed at me, a voice shouted, "How old?" My answer came, "Eighteen." The cane shoved me aside. Like a puppet I went. I knew Mama was marching on—in the opposite direction. I did not turn around. I could not. I knew she was looking at me as Papa had looked at us from the platform of the train. I knew that if I turned around we would have to run to each other—and that they would beat us or shoot us. We had to go on alone.

I was herded toward a group where my friends Ilse, Rita, and Ruth stood. Our parents were led to the other side of the meadow where a barbed wire enclosure had been set up. I did not see Mama, but we saw how earrings were torn out of ears, rings from fingers, and all thrown into a pail. I pictured Mama's wide wedding band with Papa's inscription in it among them, and I pictured the SS men digging greedily into the gold. Digging into people's love and pledges. . . .

I saw a couple we knew. With their baby in their arms they walked up to the SS man, the judge of life and death. He told them to give the baby to those marching to the right, and motioned them to the group to the left. I

VOCABULARY
security—safety.
enclosure—fenced area.
inscription—letters or writing on something, such as a ring or trophy.
pledges—promises, especially wedding vows.

"Good-bye" CONTINUED

saw the couple look at each other. Then I turned away, feeling the wide field revolving around me. When I looked again, sick and limp, I saw the couple <u>embracing</u> their baby—and walking slowly toward the right. . . .

We had assumed all along that we were going on a train, but now a truck came for us. I was the last one to enter it. Then I screamed, "I want to go to my mother!" and jumped down. Just then Merin passed. He looked at me, and with strength unsuspected in that little man, he picked me up and threw me back on the truck.

"You are too young to die," he said tonelessly.

I glared at him. "I hate you," I screamed. "I hate you!"

His eyes were without expression; there was a faint smile on his pale thin lips. It would have been easy for him to order me down and send me with my mother. Why did he not? Strange that the man who sent my mother to death had pushed me into the arms of life!

Someone fastened the <u>canvas</u> across the back of the truck and Merin walked away. Then above all the screams coming from behind the barbed wire I heard my mother. "Where to?" she called. I spread my arms and leaned out of the truck. I did not know the answer.

"Mama! Mama!" I called, as if the word could convey all I felt. Above all the confused, painful cries I heard Mama's voice again.

"Be strong!" And I heard it again like an echo: "Be strong." Those were my mother's last words to me.

STOP aND REFLECT

Review the predictions you made while reading. Which of them turned out to be true?

_____

_____

_____

VOCABULARY
embracing—holding tightly.
canvas—heavy fabric or cloth used to cover things.

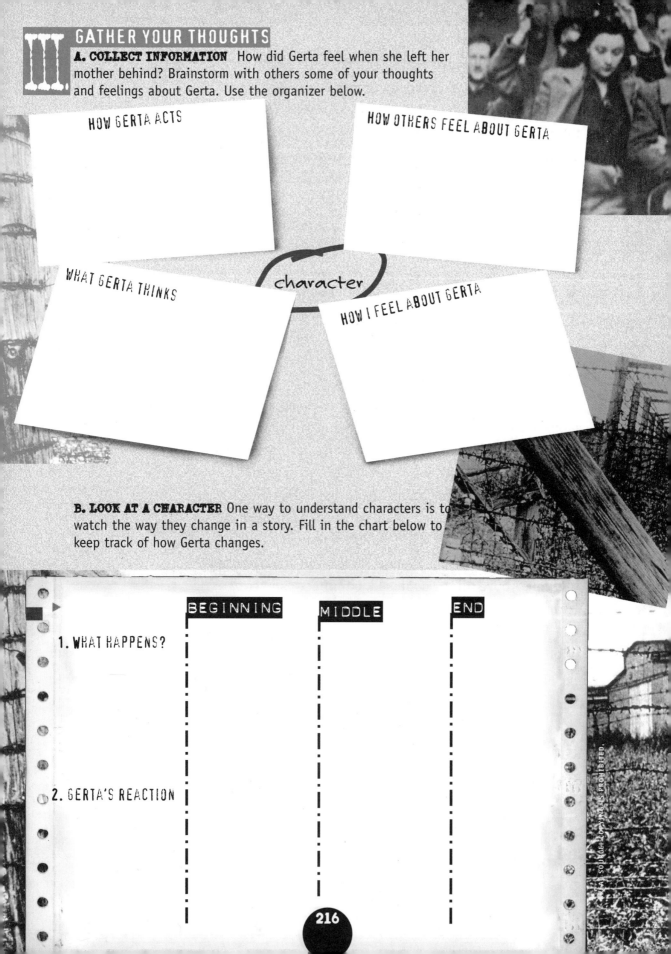

GATHER YOUR THOUGHTS

A. COLLECT INFORMATION How did Gerta feel when she left her mother behind? Brainstorm with others some of your thoughts and feelings about Gerta. Use the organizer below.

HOW GERTA ACTS

HOW OTHERS FEEL ABOUT GERTA

WHAT GERTA THINKS

character

HOW I FEEL ABOUT GERTA

B. LOOK AT A CHARACTER One way to understand characters is to watch the way they change in a story. Fill in the chart below to keep track of how Gerta changes.

	BEGINNING	MIDDLE	END
1. WHAT HAPPENS?			
2. GERTA'S REACTION			

COPYING IS PROHIBITED.

IV. WRITE

Write a **journal entry** for Gerta. Imagine that it is the night after she has said her good-byes to her mother and father.

1. Write in the first person—that is, use *I* instead of *she*.

2. Use the Writers' Checklist to help you revise.

WRITERS' CHECKLIST

CONFUSING PAIRS

<u>They're</u> means "they are."

❑ Did you make sure you used <u>they're</u> and <u>their</u> correctly? EXAMPLE: *They're coming for us now. Their parents are gone.*

<u>It's</u> means "it is."

❑ Did you make sure you used <u>it's</u> and <u>its</u> correctly? EXAMPLE: *It's time to go. The train is on its way.*

Do you like the writing style of Gerta Weismann Klein's memoir? Why or why not?

Kurt Vonnegut

Kurt Vonnegut

Kurt Vonnegut (1922–) has written a variety of novels, plays, essays, and short stories. Many of his best-known works, including the novel *Slaughterhouse-Five* and the short stories in *Welcome to the Monkey House,* blend science fiction and fantasy and mix serious themes with humor.

BY THE BEST SELLING AUTHOR OF TIMEQUAKE

KURT VONNEGUT

WELCOME TO THE MONKEY HOUSE

"VONNEGUT IS GEORGE ORWELL, DR. CALIGARI AND FLASH GORDON COMPOUNDED INTO ONE WRITER... A ZANY BUT MORAL MAD SCIENTIST." –*Time*

23: Harrison Bergeron

You probably know more than you think you do. Sometimes thinking about key words can help you prepare for reading. A good reader looks at a piece of writing and asks: *What do I know about this topic already?*

BEFORE YOU READ

Read the first paragraph of "Harrison Bergeron" below.

1. As you read, think to yourself: What is the main idea of this story?

"Harrison Bergeron" by Kurt Vonnegut

The year was 2081, and everybody was finally equal. They weren't only equal before God and the law. They were equal every which way. Nobody was smarter than anybody else. Nobody was better looking than anybody else. Nobody was stronger or quicker than anybody else. All this equality was due to the 211th, 212th, and 213th Amendments to the Constitution, and to the unceasing vigilance of agents of the United States Handicapper General.

VOCABULARY

Amendments—changes made in a law or a document.
Constitution—written set of basic principles by which the United States is governed.
vigilance—caution; watchfulness.

2. The paragraph repeats the words *equal* and *equality*. Explore your own ideas about these concepts. Create a word web. On the lines from the center, write down words, phrases, examples, or images you associate with equality.

equality

WORD WEB

READ

As you read, keep your ideas about equality in the back of your mind.

1. Underline or circle words and phrases that seem important.

2. To help **visualize** what is going on, make sketches in the Response Notes.

3. **React** to Vonnegut's writing in the double-entry journal spaces.

"Harrison Bergeron" continued

RESPONSE NOTES

Some things about living still weren't quite right, though. April, for instance, still drove people crazy by not being springtime. And it was in that <u>clammy</u> month that the H-G men took George and Hazel Bergeron's fourteen-year-old son, Harrison, away.

It was tragic, all right, but George and Hazel couldn't think about it very hard. Hazel had a perfectly average intelligence, which meant she couldn't think about anything except in short bursts. And George, while his intelligence was way above normal, had a little mental <u>handicap</u> radio in his ear. He was required by law to wear it at all times. It was tuned to a government <u>transmitter</u>. Every twenty seconds or so, the transmitter would send out some sharp noise to keep people like George from taking unfair advantage of their brains.

George and Hazel were watching television. There were tears on Hazel's cheeks, but she'd forgotten for the moment what they were about.

On the television screen were <u>ballerinas</u>.

A buzzer sounded in George's head. His thoughts fled in panic, like bandits from a burglar alarm.

"That was a real pretty dance, that dance they just did," said Hazel.

"Huh?" said George.

"That dance—it was nice," said Hazel.

"Yup," said George. He tried to think a little about the ballerinas. They weren't really very good—no better than anybody else would have been, anyway. They

EXAMPLE:

VOCABULARY

clammy—cold and damp.
handicap—advantage or disadvantage given in a race, contest, or game so that all players have an equal chance.
transmitter—electronic device that sends signals.
ballerinas—women who dance in a ballet.

were burdened with sashweights and bags of birdshot, and their faces were masked, so that no one, seeing a free and graceful gesture or a pretty face, would feel like something the cat drug in. George was toying with the vague notion that maybe dancers shouldn't be handicapped. But he didn't get very far with it before another noise in his ear radio scattered his thoughts.

George winced. So did two out of the eight ballerinas.

Hazel saw him wince. Having no mental handicap herself, she had to ask George what the latest sound had been.

"Sounded like somebody hitting a milk bottle with a ball peen hammer," said George.

"I'd think it would be real interesting, hearing all the different sounds," said Hazel, a little envious. "All the things they think up."

"Um," said George.

DOUBLE-ENTRY JOURNAL

QUOTES	MY THOUGHTS
EXAMPLE: "George was toying with the vague notion that maybe dancers shouldn't be handicapped."	Wonder what this is? Isn't this sort of crazy?
"Having no mental handicap herself. . . . 'I'd think it would be real interesting, hearing all the different sounds,' said Hazel. . . ."	

VOCABULARY
burdened—weighed down.
sashweights—weights used in the sides of windows to make them go up and down easily.
birdshot—small, heavy metal balls used in shotgun shells.
winced—draw back out of pain.
ball peen hammer—tool with a narrow, pointed metal head.
envious—showing disappointment because someone else has what you want.

"Only, if I was Handicapper General, you know what I would do?" said Hazel. Hazel, as a matter of fact, bore a strong resemblance to the Handicapper General, a woman named Diana Moon Glampers. "If I was Diana Moon Glampers," said Hazel, "I'd have chimes on Sunday—just chimes. Kind of in honor of religion."

"I could think, if it was just chimes," said George.

"Well—maybe make 'em real loud," said Hazel. "I think I'd make a good Handicapper General."

"Good as anybody else," said George.

"Who knows better'n I do what normal is?" said Hazel.

"Right," said George. He began to think glimmeringly about his abnormal son who was now in jail, about Harrison, but a twenty-one-gun salute in his head stopped that.

"Boy!" said Hazel, "that was a doozy, wasn't it?"

It was such a doozy that George was white and trembling, and tears stood on the rims of his red eyes. Two of the eight ballerinas had collapsed to the studio floor, were holding their temples.

"All of a sudden you look so tired," said Hazel. "Why don't you stretch out on the sofa, so's you can rest your handicap bag on the pillows, honeybunch." She was referring to the forty-seven pounds of birdshot in a canvas bag, which was padlocked around George's neck. "Go on and rest the bag for a little while," she said. "I don't care if you're not equal to me for a while."

DOUBLE-ENTRY JOURNAL

QUOTE	MY THOUGHTS
"I don't care if you're not equal to me for a while."	

VOCABULARY
resemblance—likeness.
chimes—musical sounds made by a set of bells.
salute—honor in a formal manner by firing off guns.
doozy—something extraordinary or bizarre.
padlocked—held or fastened securely by a lock.

RESPONSE NOTES

George weighed the bag with his hands. "I don't mind it," he said. "I don't notice it any more. It's just a part of me."

"You been so tired lately—kind of wore out," said Hazel. "If there was just some way we could make a little hole in the bottom of the bag, and just take out a few of them lead balls. Just a few."

"Two years in prison and two thousand dollars fine for every ball I took out," said George. "I don't call that a bargain."

"If you could just take a few out when you came home from work," said Hazel. "I mean—you don't compete with anybody around here. You just set around."

"If I tried to get away with it," said George, "then other people'd get away with it—and pretty soon we'd be right back to the dark ages again, with everybody competing against everybody else. You wouldn't like that, would you?"

"I'd hate it," said Hazel.

"There you are," said George. The minute people start cheating on laws, what do you think happens to society?"

If Hazel hadn't been able to come up with an answer to this question, George couldn't have supplied one. A siren was going off in his head.

"Reckon it'd fall all apart," said Hazel.

"What would?" said George blankly.

Society," said Hazel uncertainly. "Wasn't that what you just said?"

"Who knows?" said George.

DOUBLE-ENTRY JOURNAL

QUOTE	MY THOUGHTS
"The minute people start cheating on laws, what do you think happens to society?"	

GATHER YOUR THOUGHTS

A. STATE THE MAIN IDEA What point do you think Kurt Vonnegut is trying to make in this story? Write what you believe is the main idea of "Harrison Bergeron."

The story "Harrison Bergeron" shows that equality is

B. SUPPORT THE MAIN IDEA Go back to the story and find events and quotes that support your main idea statement. Record them and your thoughts about them in the organizer below.

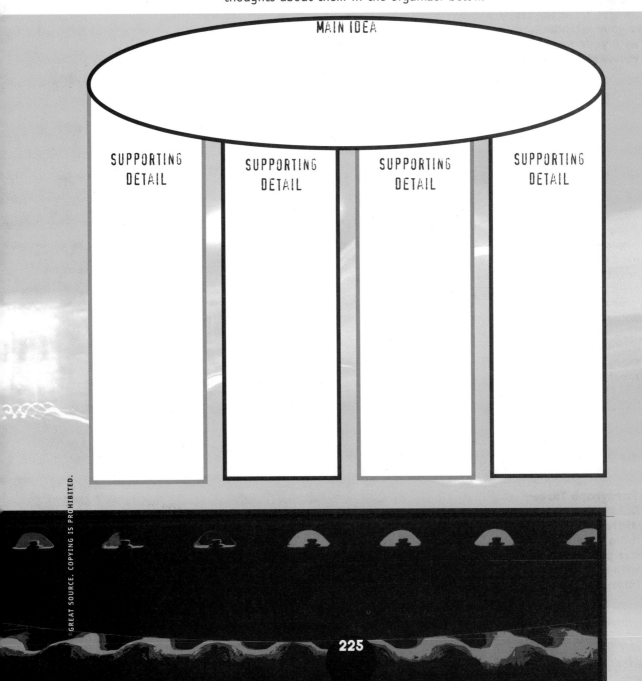

MAIN IDEA

SUPPORTING DETAIL

SUPPORTING DETAIL

SUPPORTING DETAIL

SUPPORTING DETAIL

IV. WRITE

Turn your ideas into a **3-paragraph essay**. Your essay needs to answer the question: *What does "Harrison Bergeron" say about equality?*

1. Answer the question and use specific ideas from the story to support your answer.

2. After you write, use the Writers' Checklist to revise.

Paragraph One—Introduction

Get your readers' attention. For this essay, you could include some striking images from the story. End your introduction with your main idea, or thesis statement.

Paragraph Two—Body

Develop and support your idea using specific details from the selection.

Organize your details in an order that makes sense, such as from beginning to end of the story or from least to most important.

Paragraph Three—Conclusion

Restate your thesis, or main idea.

Leave your readers with a strong impression.

V. WRAP-UP

How would you rate this story? Would you recommend the story? Explain why.

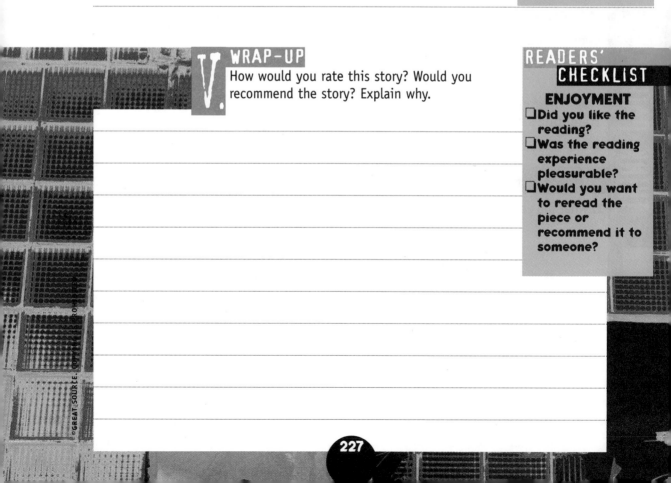

©GREAT SOURCE. COPYING IS PROHIBITED.

Have you ever heard the saying "There's strength in numbers"? That saying means that some things are easier to do when you have help. That's true when you read, too. If you work with another reader, you have a chance to ask questions and "bounce ideas" off each other. While you are helping someone else understand a piece of writing, you will also be clarifying your own ideas.

I. BEFORE YOU READ

Pair up with a partner. Read one of the sentences below to your partner. Then ask him or her to read you one. Go through them all. Talk about what this story might be about and answer the questions below.

THINK-PAIR-AND-SHARE

"Isn't there anything you care about but ripping, hacking, bending, rending, smashing, and bashing?"

"You take away his boots and give him a horn, and I'm not supposed to get curious?" he said.

"It's all over with Jim and me," said Quinn. "Last night was the payoff. I'm sending him back where he came from."

A small cry of despair came from Jim Donnini. It was meant to be private, but it pierced every ear with its poignancy.

Hemholtz stepped onto the podium, and rattled his baton against his music stand.

1. What did you learn about the story by sharing these sentences?

_____

_____

2. Who are some of the characters in the story?

_____

3. What do you think this story is about?

_____

_____

_____

_____

READ

Stay with your partner. Take turns reading aloud, trading off after each paragraph or two.

1. Pause when either one of you needs help or has a guess about what will happen.

2. As you read, jot down your **questions** and **predictions** in the Response Notes.

[*At this point in the story, Jim Donnini, a boy with a troubled past, has gone to live with his step-mom's brother, Bert Quinn. George Helmholtz, a music teacher, is Quinn's friend.*]

"The Kid Nobody Could Handle"
by Kurt Vonnegut

Helmholtz suddenly dropped the telephone into its cradle before the principal could answer. "Isn't there anything you care about but ripping, hacking, bending, <u>rending</u>, smashing, bashing?" he cried. "Anything? Anything but those boots?"

"Go on! Call up whoever you're gonna call," said Jim.

Helmholtz opened a locker and took a <u>trumpet</u> from it. He thrust the trumpet into Jim's arms. "There!" he said, puffing with emotion. "There's my treasure. It's the dearest thing I own. I give it to you to smash. I won't move a muscle to stop you. You can have the added pleasure of watching my heart break while you do it."

Jim looked at him oddly. He laid down the trumpet.

"Go on!" said Helmholtz. "If the world has treated you so badly, it deserves to have the trumpet smashed!"

"I—" said Jim. Helmholtz grabbed his belt, put a foot behind him, and dumped him on the floor.

Helmholtz pulled Jim's boots off and threw them into a corner. "There!" said Helmholtz savagely. He jerked the boy to his feet again and thrust the trumpet into his arms once more.

Jim Donnini was barefoot now. He had lost his socks with his boots. The boy looked down. The feet that had

EXAMPLE:
Why are the boots so important to him?

VOCABULARY
rending—pulling apart violently; tearing.
trumpet—brass musical instrument with a strong tone.

once seemed big black clubs were narrow as chicken wings now—bony and blue, and not quite clean.

The boy shivered, then quaked. Each quake seemed to shake something loose inside, until, at last, there was no boy left. No boy at all. Jim's head lolled, as though he waited only for death.

PREDICT PREDICT

What do you think Jim will do with the trumpet?

....

....

....

PREDICT PREDICT

Helmholtz was overwhelmed by <u>remorse</u>. He threw his arms around the boy. "Jim! Jim—listen to me, boy!"

Jim stopped quaking.

"You know what you've got there—the trumpet?" said Helmholtz. "You know what's special about it?"

Jim only sighed.

"It belonged to <u>John Philip Sousa</u>!" said Helmholtz. He rocked and shook Jim gently, trying to bring him back to life. "I'll trade it to you, Jim—for your boots. It's yours, Jim! John Philip Sousa's trumpet is yours! It's worth hundreds of dollars, Jim—thousands!"

Jim laid his head on Helmholtz's breast.

"It's better than boots, Jim," said Helmholtz. "You can learn to play it. You're somebody, Jim. You're the boy with John Philip Sousa's trumpet!"

Helmholtz released Jim slowly, sure the boy would topple. Jim didn't fall. He stood alone. The trumpet was still in his arms.

VOCABULARY
remorse—deep, painful regret for having done wrong.
John Philip Sousa—a famous American music conductor (1854-1932), who wrote
    such march songs as *Stars and Stripes Forever*.

"I'll take you home, Jim," said Helmholtz. "Be a good boy and I won't say a word about tonight. Polish your trumpet, and learn to be a good boy."

"Can I have my boots?" said Jim dully.

"No," said Helmholtz. "I don't think they're good for you."

He drove Jim home. He opened the car windows and the air seemed to refresh the boy. He let him out at Quinn's restaurant. The soft pats of Jim's bare feet on the sidewalk echoed down the empty street. He climbed through a window, and into his bedroom behind the kitchen. And all was still.

The next morning the <u>waddling</u> clanking, muddy machines were making the vision of Bert Quinn come true. They were smoothing off the place where the hill had been behind the restaurant. They were making it as level as a <u>billiard table</u>.

Helmholtz sat in a booth again. Quinn joined him again. Jim mopped again. Jim kept his eyes down, refusing to notice Helmholtz. And he didn't seem to care when a surf of suds broke over the toes of his small and narrow brown <u>Oxfords</u>.

"Eating out two mornings in a row—" said Quinn. "Something wrong at home?"

"My wife's still out of town," said Helmholtz.

"While the cat's away—" said Quinn. He winked.

"When the cat's away," said Helmholtz, "this mouse gets lonesome."

Quinn leaned forward. "Is that what got you out of bed in the middle of the night, Helmholtz? Loneliness?" He jerked his head at Jim. "Kid! Go get Mr. Helmholtz his horn."

VOCABULARY

waddling—walking with short steps and an awkward, swaying motion.
billiard table—flat table for playing pool.
Oxfords—type of dressy shoes (as opposed to his bicycle boots).

How has Helmholtz tried to help Jim?

....

....

....

Jim raised his head, and Helmholtz saw that his eyes were oysterlike again. He marched away to get the trumpet.

Quinn now showed that he was excited and angry. "You take away his boots and give him a horn, and I'm not supposed to get curious?" he said. "I'm not supposed to start asking questions? I'm not supposed to find out you caught him taking the school apart? You'd make a lousy crook, Helmholtz. You'd leave your baton, sheet music, and your driver's license at the scene of the crime."

"I don't think about hiding clues," said Helmholtz. "I just do what I do. I was going to tell you."

Quinn's feet danced and his shoes squeaked like mice. "Yes?" he said. "Well, I've got some news for you too."

"What is that?" said Helmholtz uneasily.

"It's all over with Jim and me," said Quinn. "Last night was the payoff. I'm sending him back where he came from.

"To another string of foster homes?" said Helmholtz weakly.

"Whatever the experts figure out to do with a kid like that." Quinn sat back, exhaled noisily, and went limp with relief.

"You can't," said Helmholtz.

"I can," said Quinn.

"That will be the end of him," said Helmholtz. "He

VOCABULARY
baton—light stick or wand used by a leader of a band or orchestra.
sheet music—printed music on sheets of paper.

can't stand to be thrown away like that one more time."

"He can't feel anything," said Quinn. "I can't help him; I can't hurt him. Nobody can. There isn't a nerve in him."

"A bundle of scar tissue," said Helmholtz.

The bundle of <u>scar</u> tissue returned with the trumpet. <u>Impassively</u>, he laid it on the table in front of Helmholtz.

Helmholtz forced a smile. "It's yours, Jim," he said. "I gave it to you."

"Take it while you got the chance, Helmholtz," said Quinn. "He doesn't want it. All he'll do is swap it for a knife or a pack of cigarettes."

"He doesn't know what it is, yet," said Helmholtz. "It takes a while to find out."

"Is it any good?" said Quinn.

"Any good?" said Helmholtz, not believing his ears. "Any good?" He didn't see how anyone could look at the instrument and not be warmed and dazzled by it. "Any good?" he murmured. "It belonged to John Philip Sousa."

Quinn blinked stupidly. "Who?"

Helmholtz's hands fluttered on the table top like the wings of a dying bird. "Who was John Philip Sousa?" he piped. No more words came. The subject was too big for a tired man to cover. The dying bird <u>expired</u> and lay still.

After a long silence, Helmholtz picked up the trumpet. He kissed the cold mouthpiece and

VOCABULARY
scar—mark left by a healed cut or wound.
Impassively—without feeling or emotion.
expired—died.

pumped the valves in a dream of a brilliant <u>cadenza</u>. Over the bell of the instrument, Helmholtz saw Jim Donnini's face, seemingly floating in space—all but deaf and blind. Now Helmholtz saw the futility of men and their treasures. He had thought that his greatest treasure, the trumpet, could buy a soul for Jim. The trumpet was worthless.

Deliberately, Helmholtz hammered the trumpet against the table edge. He bent it around a coat tree. He handed the wreck to Quinn.

"Ya busted it," said Quinn, amazed. "Why'dja do that? What's that prove?"

"I—I don't know," said Helmholtz. A terrible

CLARIFY

Think about what happened. If this trumpet is important to Helmholtz, why did he break it?

....

....

CLARIFY

<u>blasphemy</u> rumbled deep in him, like the warning of a volcano. And then, <u>irresistibly</u>, out it came. "Life is no damn good," said Helmholtz. His face twisted as he fought back tears and shame.

Helmholtz, the mountain that walked like a man, was falling apart. Jim Donnini's eyes filled with pity and alarm. They came alive. They became human. Helmholtz had got a message through. Quinn looked at Jim, and something like hope flickered for the first time in his bitterly lonely old face.

Two weeks later, a new semester began at Lincoln High.

In the band rehearsal room, the members of C Band were waiting for their leader—were waiting for their destinies as musicians to unfold.

VOCABULARY
cadenza—showy part or flourish, often at the end, in a musical work.
blasphemy—abuse or hatred of God or sacred things.
irresistibly—not able to be withstood or resisted; overwhelming.

Helmholtz stepped onto the podium, and rattled his baton against his music stand. "The Voices of Spring," he said. "Everybody hear that? The Voices of Spring?"

There were rustling sounds as the musicians put the music on their stands. In the pregnant silence that followed their readiness, Helmholtz glanced at Jim Donnini, who sat on the last seat of the worst trumpet section of the worst band in school.

His trumpet, John Philip Sousa's trumpet, George M. Helmholtz's trumpet, had been repaired.

"Think of it this way," said Helmholtz. "Our aim is to make the world more beautiful than it was when we came into it. It can be done. You can do it."

A small cry of despair came from Jim Donnini. It was meant to be private, but it pierced every ear with its poignancy.

"How?" said Jim.

"Love yourself," said Helmholtz, "and make your instrument sing about it. A-one, a-two, a-three." Down came his baton.

VOCABULARY
pregnant—meaningful; significant.

SUMMARIZE SUMMARIZE SUMMARIZE SUMMARIZE

How would you explain in your own words what Jim is feeling at the end?

....

....

....

....

....

....

....

....

GATHER YOUR THOUGHTS

A. USE A STORY MAP One way to help you remember what you read is to organize the information right after you read. Use the Story Map below to gather the key information from the story.

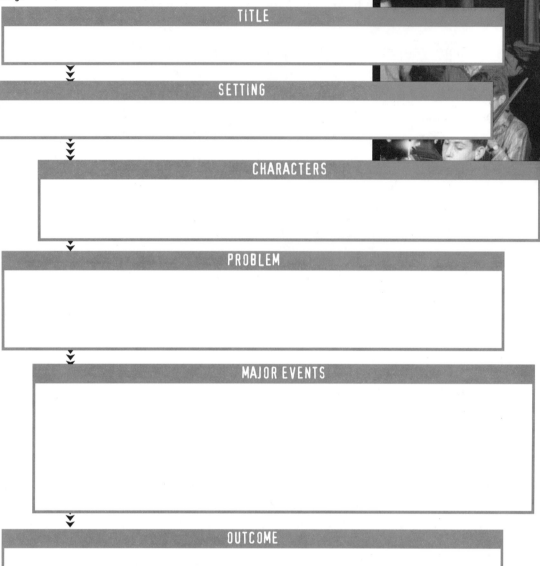

STORY MAP

TITLE

SETTING

CHARACTERS

PROBLEM

MAJOR EVENTS

OUTCOME

B. QUICKWRITE Now think about what will happen next to Jim Donnini. What will he do? Where will he go? Brainstorm several ideas for another episode about Jim that you could write.

IV. WRITE

Create an **episode** about Jim.
1. Use your ideas from the previous page to help you plan the action.
2. Use the Writers' Checklist on the next page to help you revise.

First sentence— start at the beginning. Set the scene.

Use chronological order—tell the events from beginning to end.

Continue your writing on the next page.

Continue your writing from the previous page.

V. WRAP-UP

What made this story difficult or easy to read? Explain what strategies you used to understand the story.

Acknowledgments

13 "The Good Daughter" by Caroline Hwang. Reprinted by permission of Caroline Hwang.

22 "Bridges" by Walter Dean Myers. Reprinted by permission of Walter Dean Myers.

35 "Pilots' Reflections" by Manfred von Richthofen. Reprinted by permission of Brig. General Stanley Ulanoff.

43 "Adventures of the U-202" by Baron Speigel. Excerpt from *The Adventures of the U-202* by Baron Spiegel of Peckelsheim.

50 "you're being so good, so kind," from *Maud Martha* by Gwendolyn Brooks. Excerpt from MAUD MARTHA by Gwendolyn Brooks, published by Third World Press. Copyright © 1953 by Gwendolyn Brooks Blakely.

57 "Maud Martha and New York," from *Maud Martha* by Gwendolyn Brooks. Excerpt from MAUD MARTHA by Gwendolyn Brooks, published by Third World Press. Copyright © 1953 by Gwendolyn Brooks Blakely.

67 "Legal Alien" by Pat Mora. "Legal Alien" by Pat Mora is reprinted with permission from the publisher of *Chants* (Houston: Arte Público Press—University of Houston, 1985).

69 "Immigrants" by Pat Mora is reprinted with permission from the publisher of *Borders* (Houston: Arte Público Press—University of Houston, 1985).

74 "A Simple Proposition," from *Who's Hu?* by Lensey Namioka. Excerpt from WHO'S HU? by Lensey Namioka. Copyright © 1980 by Lensey Namioka.

86 "The Cyclops' Cave" by Bernard Evslin. Reprinted by arrangement with Writers House, Inc. as agent for the proprietor. Copyright 1999 by William Morrow.

100 "Hercules" by Edith Hamilton. From MYTHOLOGY by Edith Hamilton. Copyright 1942 by Edith Hamilton; Copyright © renewed 1969 by Dorian Fielding Reid and Doris Fielding Reid. By permission of Little, Brown and Company.

113, 120 "The Richer, the Poorer" by Dorothy West. From THE RICHER, THE POORER by Dorothy West. Copyright © 1995 by Dorothy West. Used by permission of Doubleday, a division of Random House, Inc.

126 "Animals Unite!," from *Animal Farm* by George Orwell. Excerpt from ANIMAL FARM by George Orwell. Copyright 1946 by Harcourt, Inc. and renewed 1974 by Sonia Orwell. Reprinted by permission of the publisher.

137 "The Fast," from *An Autobiography* by Mohandas Gandhi. Excerpt from AN AUTOBIOGRAPHY by Mahatma Gandhi. Reprinted by permission of the Navajivan Trust.

147 "A Sea of Dunes" by Jim Brandenburg. From SAND AND FOG. Copyright © 1994 by Jim Brandenburg. Reprinted with permission from Walker and Company, 435 Hudson Street, New York, New York 10014. All Rights Reserved.

154 "The Widows of the Reserves" by Phyllis P. Ntantala. Reprinted by permission of the author, Phyllis P. Ntantala.

162, 172 "Ramiro," from *Always Running* by Luis Rodriguez. Excerpt from ALWAYS RUNNING by Luis Rodriguez (Curbstone Press, 1993). Reprinted with permission of Curbstone Press.

179 "Refusing Service," from *Dust Tracks on a Road* by Zora Neale Hurston. Excerpt (pages 162-165) from DUST TRACKS ON A ROAD by Zora Neale Hurston. Copyright 1942 by Zora Neale Hurston. Copyright renewed 1970 by John C. Hurston. Reprinted by permission of HarperCollins Publishers, Inc.

188 "Time to Look and Listen" by Magdoline Asfahani. Reprinted by permission of Magdoline Asfahani.

198 "A Soldier's Letter Home" by Delbert Cooper. Reprinted by permission of the Museum of Jewish Heritage.

207 "Good-bye," from *All But My Life* by Gerta Weissmann Klein. Excerpt from ALL BUT MY LIFE by Gerta Weissmann Klein. Copyright © 1957 by Gerta Weissmann Klein. Renewed copyright © 1985 by Gerta Weissmann Klein. Reprinted by permission of Hill and Wang, a division of Farrar, Straus & Giroux, Inc.

220 "Harrison Bergeron" by Kurt Vonnegut. "Harrison Bergeron" by Kurt Vonnegut, from WELCOME TO THE MONKEY HOUSE by Kurt Vonnegut, Jr. Copyright © 1961 by Kurt Vonnegut, Jr. Used by permission of Delacorte Press/Seymour Lawrence, a division of Random House, Inc.

229 "The Kid Nobody Could Handle" by Kurt Vonnegut. "The Kid Nobody Could Handle by Kurt Vonnegut, from WELCOME TO THE MONKEY HOUSE by Kurt Vonnegut, Jr. Copyright ©1961 by Kurt Vonnegut, Jr. Used by permission of Delacorte Press/Seymour Lawrence, a division of Random House, Inc.

Photography:

COVER: All photos © Eileen Ryan.

TABLE OF CONTENTS: All photos © Eileen Ryan except backgrounds—courtesy Library of Congress.

INTRODUCTION: All photos © Eileen Ryan.

CHAPTER 1: All photos © Eileen Ryan except where noted. Page 11: upper right—courtesy Library of Congress. Page 24: courtesy Library of Congress. Page 29: inset—courtesy Library of Congress.

CHAPTER 2: All photos courtesy Library of Congress except were noted. Page 33: center right—courtesy National Archive. Page 42: upper right—© Eileen Ryan, center left—courtesy National Archive. Page 44: lower left—courtesy National Archive. Page 45: center, lower right—courtesy National Archive. Page 46: courtesy National Archive. Page 48: © Eileen Ryan

CHAPTER 3: All photos © Eileen Ryan except where noted. Page 49: center—courtesy Library of Congress, lower left—Maud

Acknowledgments continued

Martha © Gwendolyn Brooks Blakely, Third World Press, May 1993.

CHAPTER 4: All photos © Eileen Ryan except where noted. Page 65: center right—courtesy Library of Congress.

CHAPTER 5: All photos © Eileen Ryan except where noted. Page 85: courtesy Library of Congress. Page 86: center left—courtesy Library of Congress. Page 91: courtesy Library of Congress. Page 93: courtesy Library of Congress. Page 97: upper right—courtesy Library of Congress. Pages 98-99: courtesy Library of Congress. Page 108: upper left—courtesy Library of Congress.

CHAPTER 6: All photos © Eileen Ryan except where noted. Page 111: top—© Alison Shaw, upper right—© by permission of Doubleday, a division of Random House, Inc., center—© Eileen Ryan, lower two—courtesy Library of Congress. Page 113: upper right—courtesy Library of Congress. Page 115: lower right—courtesy Library of Congress. Page 122: courtesy Library of Congress.

CHAPTER 7: All photos © Eileen Ryan except where noted. Page 125: courtesy Library of Congress. Page 126: upper right—courtesy Library of Congress. Page 129: center left—courtesy Library of Congress. Page 133: courtesy Library of Congress. Page 134: upper right—courtesy Library of Congress. Page 135: background—courtesy Library of Congress. Page 136: upper right—courtesy Library of Congress. Page 139: courtesy Library of Congress. Page 140: lower left—courtesy Library of Congress. Page 142: courtesy Library of Congress. Page 144: Library of Congress.

CHAPTER 8: All photos courtesy Library of Congress except were noted. Page 145: Al Myers; upper right—courtesy National Archive. Page 146: upper right—courtesy National Archive. Page 148: © Jason Lauré. Page 149: center right—© Jason Lauré. Page 150: courtesy National Archive. Pages 153-6: Al Myers. Page 158: Al Myers. Page 159: courtesy National Archive. Page 160: Al Meyers.

CHAPTER 9: All photos © Eileen Ryan except where noted. Page 161: center—courtesy of Luis Rodriguez, book cover—cover design by Stone Graphics. Used by permission of Curbstone press

CHAPTER 10: All photos courtesy Library of Congress except were noted. Pages 180-1: © Eileen Ryan. Page 184: lower right—© Eileen Ryan. Page 185: background—© Eileen Ryan. Page 186: lower right—© Eileen Ryan. Pages 191: courtesy National Archive. Page 196: © Eileen Ryan, background—courtesy National Archive.

CHAPTER 11: All photos courtesy Library of Congress.

CHAPTER 12: All photos © Eileen Ryan except where noted. Page 219: center—© Frank Capri/Archive Photos, lower right—© Used by permission of Delacorte Press/Seymour Lawrence, a division of Random House, Inc. Page 220: courtesy Library of Congress. Page 225: upper right—courtesy Library of Congress. Page 230: lower left—courtesy Library of Congress. Page 233: lower right—courtesy Library of Congress. Page 237: upper right—courtesy Library of Congress. Page 238: upper right—courtesy Library of Congress.

Cover and Book Design:
Christine Ronan and Sean O'Neill, Ronan Design

Permissions:
Feldman and Associates

Developed by Nieman Inc.

Author/Title **Index**

"Adventures of the U-202," 43
"Ain't I a Woman?," 8
All But My Life, 207
Always Running, 162, 172
Autobiography, An 137
Animal Farm, 126
"Animals Unite!," 126
Asfahani, Magdoline, 188
Brandenburg, Jim, 147
"Bridges," 22
Brooks, Gwendolyn, 50, 57
Cooper, Delbert, 198
"Cyclops' Cave, The," 86
Dust Tracks on a Road, 179
Evslin, Bernard, 86
"Fast, The," 137
Franklin, Benjamin, 10
Gandhi, Mohandas K., 137
"Good-bye," 207
"Good Daughter, The," 13
Hamilton, Edith, 100
"Harrison Bergeron," 220
"Hercules," 100
Hull, Robert, 35
Hurston, Zora Neale, 179
Hwang, Caroline, 13
"Immigrants," 69
"Kid Nobody Could Handle, The," 229
Klein, Gerta Weismann, 207
"Legal Alien," 67
"Letter to Samuel Mather," 10
Maud Martha, 50, 57
"Maud Martha and New York," 57
Mora, Pat, 67, 69
Myers, Walter Dean, 22
Namioka, Lensey, 74
Ntantala, Phyllis, 154
Orwell, George, 126
"Pilots' Reflections," 35
"Ramiro," 162, 172
"Refusing Service," 179
"Richer, the Poorer, The," 113, 120
Rodriguez, Luis, 162, 172
"Sea of Dunes, A," 147
"Simple Proposition, A," 74
"Soldier's Letter Home, A" 198
Spiegel, Baron, 43
"Time to Look and Listen," 188
Truth, Sojourner, 8
Vonnegut, Kurt, 220, 229
West, Dorothy, 113, 120
Who's Hu, 74
"Widows of the Reserves, The," 154
"you're being so good, so kind," 50